Designer-Drug Abuse

Designer-Drug Abuse

MICHELE McCORMICK

An Impact Book
New York/London/Toronto/Sydney
Franklin Watts/1989

Photographs courtesy of:
Gamma/Liaison: pp. 14 (Gregg Smith), 104 (Raymond Piat);
CDC: p. 17 (both); DEA: pp. 23, 55, 63, 75, 78, 81;
University of California at Davis, School of Medicine:
p. 31; Monkmeyer: p. 37; Wide World Photos: pp. 42, 49,
67, 73, 90 (both); Picture Group: p. 98 (Mark Richards).

Library of Congress Cataloging-in-Publication Data

McCormick, Michele.
Designer-drug abuse / by Michele McCormick
p.   cm.—(An Impact book)
Bibliography: p.
Includes index.
Summary: Explains what designer drugs are and how they are
different from other drugs, such as cocaine: and discusses their
effects on the mind and body, how they are made and distributed,
and laws regarding these drugs.
ISBN 0-531-10660-8
1. Drug abuse—United States—Juvenile literature.   2. Designer
drugs—United States—Juvenile literature.   3. Narcotics, Control
of—United States—Juvenile literature.   [1. Drug abuse.
2. Designer drugs.]   I. Title.
HV5825.M36   1989
362.2'93—dc19   88-30450   CIP   AC

Contents

Designer-Drug Abuse

Acknowledgments

This book would not have been possible without the help of a number of people and organizations. In particular, I'd like to thank

Mim Landry, of the Haight-Ashbury Free Medical Clinic; Dr. Gary Henderson, associate professor of pharmacology at the University of California at Davis; Pat Gregory, of the Drug Enforcement Agency; and Dan Largent, of California's Bureau of Narcotics Enforcement. All of these people were extremely generous with their time, and more than willing to share their expertise.

I'd also like to thank Ben Neff, a now-retired administrator with the Sacramento School District, and Lynn Pribus, my friend. Their comments on the manuscript were invaluable.

Finally, I extend my appreciation to Henry Rasof, my editor. The importance of his role in shaping this material cannot be overemphasized.

1
What Are Designer Drugs?

Imagine a street drug one thousand times more powerful than heroin. It is so strong that an amount barely larger than a single crystal of salt is a lethal dose. It is so fast-acting that users who injected it have been found dead with the needle still in their veins. Its presence is so difficult to detect that only a handful of laboratories in America are capable of doing so.

This drug is 3-methylfentanyl, a synthetic narcotic whose effects closely mimic those of heroin. Sometimes known as China White, it is a drug which exists not just in imagination, but on the streets where illicit drugs are bought and sold. It is manufactured by renegade chemists in clandestine laboratories. And, what is most remarkable and frightening, when it first surfaced in the drug culture in the early 1980s, it was perfectly legal.

A New Drug-Abuse Problem

The appearance of 3-methylfentanyl among street users was especially alarming. It was just as addictive as heroin or morphine. Its tremendous potency meant that over-doses were likely. But even more importantly, the arrival of this particular drug signaled a frightening new era of drug abuse.

Until its appearance, most of the drugs on the street had been developed for medical or scientific use. Some drugs of abuse are derived from natural substances, as in the case of heroin and cocaine; others, such as phencyclidine (PCP), amphetamines, and lysergic acid diethylamide-25 (LSD-25), were manufactured for medical or scientific applications. The production of these drugs took place in carefully controlled pharmaceutical laboratories. Their effects on animals and humans were studied carefully, in order to determine what use they might have.

However, 3-methylfentanyl has no known therapeutic value. It has passed through no formal testing procedures, and it was not developed by scientists for a legitimate purpose. It was created and manufactured for the specific purpose of abuse. It was one of the first illicit substances to be known as a *designer drug*.

What Is a Designer Drug?

Designer drug is a misleading term if ever there was one. For most of us, the word *designer* brings to mind designer clothes, designer jewelry, or designer colognes. The label has come to mean quality, reliability, and status. Designer drugs have none of those characteristics. In fact, they are precisely the opposite of everything their name implies. They are treacherous products, made under uncontrolled, unhygienic circumstances. They are commonly sold under the guise of more familiar illegal substances, and their effects are often unpredictable.

What exactly is a designer drug? The term has no scientific basis whatsoever. Its definition is based on the perceptions of those who use drugs, and those who work in fighting drug abuse.

Initially, the phrase *designer drugs* referred to newly created drugs of abuse whose chemical structure had not been defined under the law. Because the law did not precisely describe these drugs, they were absolutely legal. They had been designed specifically for abuse, and for circumventing the law.

The law was soon changed to close this loophole, however. When that happened, the commonly understood definition of designer drugs expanded to include any synthetic drug that is illicitly manufactured. The most common such drugs generally fall into one of three categories —forms of amphetamines, hallucinogens, and narcotics. They include 3-methylfentanyl, methamphetamine, PCP, MDMA (3-4-methylenedioxymethamphetamine), and the many illicitly developed variations of these drugs.

Thus, heroin is not a designer drug, because although it is produced in a laboratory it is not a synthetic. Crack is not a designer drug; it's simply a form of cocaine.

Among drug abuse experts and law enforcement personnel, the term *designer drugs* has fallen into disfavor because it is misleading, and because it does not refer to any specific scientific category of drugs. In professional circles, illegally manufactured drugs are better known as controlled substance analogues, or simply illicit synthetics.

Analogues

Some of these illicit synthetics are totally new drugs, completely unknown to scientists and doctors. How is a new drug created? All drugs have precise chemical structures. When those structures are altered by changing the location of even one or two molecules, new but related drugs are created. Such compounds, "cousins" to familiar drugs, are called *analogues.*

For example, 3-methylfentanyl is closely related to fentanyl, a surgical anesthetic. The prefix *3-methyl* indicates that a methyl group, consisting of one carbon atom sur-

Chemical structures of Heroin, Fentanyl, and 3–Methylfentanyl

Heroin

Fentanyl

3–Methylfentanyl

rounded by three atoms of hydrogen, has been added to a specific position on the fentanyl molecule.

When new atoms are added to a chemical structure, or even when the existing atoms are moved about, the effects of the drug may be changed. The precise nature of those changes cannot be predicted. Experts can guess at the possibilities by using their knowledge of the way known drugs act or by studying the results of past experiments. But the only way the exact effects of a new compound or an analogue can be known is by thorough testing.

In some cases, relatively minor changes in a drug's structure may render it completely inert, so that it has no effects whatsoever. Or, an equally simple change may create a drug so unlike its parent compound that it belongs to a completely different family of drugs.

A police officer with a display of designer drugs. The chart in the background is a chemical chart; chemicals of various combinations produce designer drugs.

The ways illicitly developed analogues may affect a human being remain unknown until a person takes the drug. Such characteristics as overdose levels, toxicity, duration of the drug's action, and the course that action will take are all mysteries. The underground chemists find the answers by testing their concoctions on themselves and their friends. Such tests can prove fatal.

Pharmaceutical experimentation, both legal and illegal, has resulted in the development of many drug analogues. Methamphetamine and MDMA are both essentially analogues of amphetamine that were legally developed early in this century. Many additional illicit analogues of both drugs have since been created. 3-methylfentanyl is only one of many illicit analogues of fentanyl, all developed specifically with drug abuse in mind.

Underground Drug Production

Although the numbers and production capabilities have increased tremendously in recent years, the existence of illegal labs is not new. Underground laboratories first began to appear in the 1960s and 1970s, when pharmaceutical houses tightened control of amphetamines. The illicit labs manufactured the newly scarce amphetamines for an avid market. Some hallucinogenic drugs, such as LSD, were also produced illegally.

During the 1980s, this activity has expanded. The fact that drugs such as PCP and methamphetamine are relatively easily synthesized has made them the most common products of unskilled chemists. But the labs also turn

ABOVE: *an array of commercially prepared amphetamines.* BELOW: *analogues of amphetamines commonly mistaken for amphetamines.*

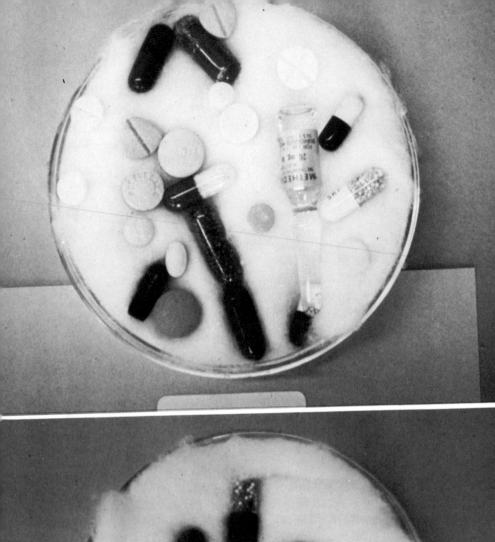
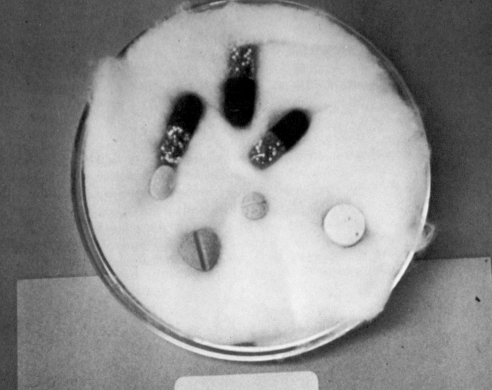

Counterfeits

out a variety of other compounds. Because this activity is clandestine and illegal, it is very difficult to monitor the emergence of experimental new substances on the street. Often their existence becomes known only when their use proves fatal or has other tragic consequences.

Who Uses Synthetics?

Synthetics are used by every category of person involved in drug abuse. Certain specific drugs have sometimes drawn a particular group of users, but generally the use then spreads into other groups.

Although some drug abusers may seek a specific synthetic, such as Ecstasy, because they have read of its effects, many of those who use synthetics have no idea what drug they are taking. To a heroin addict, for example, the fentanyl analogue is indistinguishable from real heroin. An inexperienced drug abuser might mistake the effects of methamphetamine for those of cocaine. PCP is routinely substituted for a variety of other drugs.

Some users do seek the synthetics because they are cheap or are reputed to produce a particular effect. But those who choose to use synthetics face frightening hazards. An analogue may have side effects its creator never imagined, or an unskilled chemist may accidentally create a product quite different from the one intended.

In addition to these dangers, those who use the illicit synthetics face all the hazards involved with abuse of any drug. Use of unhygienic needles carries the risk of acquired immune deficiency syndrome (AIDS), some drugs are highly addictive, the high cost of regular drug use leads many users into criminal activity, and the possession or use of these drugs is illegal and carries a jail term.

But the threat most associated with the illicit synthetics is the total uncertainty of their content and composition. The risk of overdose is extremely high. And seemingly minor laboratory mistakes can easily turn these potions into poisons.

Given all the variables, the potential dangers, and the likelihood for fatal error, it may seem surprising that the use of synthetics has not resulted in some disastrous new form of drug abuse tragedy.

As we shall see in the next chapter, it has.

2
A Chemical Bullet

Perhaps the most frightening aspect of the illicit synthetics concerns the devastating side effects they have the potential to produce. Such effects may be immediately apparent when the drug is taken, or they may appear weeks, months, even years later. They may cause death, or they may be permanently disabling.

But the precise long-term effects of the illicit synthetics are difficult to document. When an individual dies of a drug overdose, the circumstances often make it apparent what has happened. When a person develops an illness weeks or years after using an illicit drug, the cause of that illness can be nearly impossible to pinpoint.

Illicit synthetics have been linked to many health problems, the most obvious being overdose deaths. Some experts also believe there is a connection between a crippling neurological disease, Huntington's chorea, and use of illicitly manufactured drugs.[1] There is speculation that some of the new synthetics may affect the immune system and thus play a role in the development of AIDS.

Proving these theories is a complex and precise effort

that can take years. But in one case, the link between use of an illicit synthetic and the development of disease has been fully documented.

Barry Kidston

The story begins in 1976 when a college student named Barry Kidston had a bright idea. Kidston had experimented with narcotics, and he wanted to continue taking them, but he didn't want to be involved with the characters who sold them or get in trouble with the law. He needed another way to obtain the drug he wanted. He decided he would make it himself.

The drug Barry wanted to use was a heroinlike narcotic called meperidine. It is sold under the trade name Demerol, but in the United States its availability is strictly controlled.

Barry decided that he would not try to make meperidine itself, but another, similar drug not legally controlled at the time. That drug was MPPP (1-methyl-4-phenyl-4-propionoxy-piperidine).

Then twenty-three, Barry was studying chemistry at a nearby university. He succeeded in synthesizing MPPP in a small lab he set up in his basement. For six months he made his own supply. Then, that summer, while he was going through the synthesis procedure—a procedure that he must have come to regard as routine and familiar— Barry made a mistake.

An Illness Strikes

At first no one understood what had happened. All they knew was that Barry was suddenly very sick. Virtually overnight he became paralyzed. He could not move or even talk. His limbs sometimes jumped spasmodically, and he was unable to control them. It took doctors quite some time to recognize that mentally Barry was fine. His normal, alert mind was now trapped inside a body over which he no longer had control.

To doctors, the symptoms he presented were classic. He showed every sign of a well-known illness called Parkinson's disease. When Barry was given a medicine called levodopa (L-dopa), which is used to treat Parkinson's, it helped him. For a few hours at a time he could move almost normally. Then, as the L-dopa wore off, he would have to take more, or slip back into paralysis.

The doctors were mystified. Parkinson's disease is most likely to strike people sixty or older, and the symptoms usually come on extremely slowly. How had Barry, only twenty-three, fallen victim?

The Toxic Cause

Doctors got their first clue when Barry told them he had been taking a drug he had manufactured himself. They reasoned that his product may have been contaminated, or that perhaps he had made an error in the process that had resulted in the formation of a toxic substance.

In an effort to re-create Barry's actions exactly, researchers at the National Institute of Mental Health (NIMH) in Maryland obtained his detailed notes and his equipment. At that point they got lucky. They found a tiny amount of powdery residue in one of the containers Barry had used. It had to be left over from the last time he had manufactured drugs.

The substance found proved to be MPPP. What researchers didn't realize was that the MPPP had become contaminated with MPTP, a potentially toxic chemical. The MPTP (1-methyl-4-phenyl-1,2,5,6-tetrahydropyridine) had been formed because of a seemingly minor error Barry made while synthesizing MPPP. By applying too much heat at a certain point in the process, he unknowingly created a poisonous by-product.

The researchers studied the effects of MPPP on animals

*A designer-drug recipe found in an underground
lab seized by police and drug agents*

and found that it produced a temporary paralysis in rats. Unfortunately, they could do little for Barry Kidston. Although the medication L-dopa treated the effects of his disease, it was not a cure. Barry continued to abuse other drugs. Then, in 1978, he went to the grounds of the NIMH, sat down under a shady tree, took an overdose of cocaine, and died.[2]

Brain Cell Destruction

When Barry's brain was examined it was found that the cells of one area, the substantia nigra, had been destroyed. These cells are responsible for the production of a naturally occurring chemical called dopamine. Dopamine is a *neurotransmitter*—a chemical that carries messages between nerve endings in the brain. Without dopamine, a mental order to walk or wave will never reach the leg or arm.

Parkinson's disease usually occurs in older people when the cells of the substantia nigra gradually die off and the supply of dopamine is depleted. Early symptoms may be barely apparent. A Parkinson's victim may notice he is suddenly having trouble with his tennis game or other activities requiring good coordination. Gradually the difficulty in achieving normal movement progresses, perhaps over months or years, to a time when the stricken individual recognizes the fact that he must be ill.

Barry's experience was much different. The MPTP he accidentally took acted as a chemical bullet. It was drawn specifically to the dopamine-producing cells, as if by direct aim, and once it reached them it destroyed them forever.[3]

A short while after Barry's death the results of the research his illness had initiated were published in an obscure medical journal. They received little attention. The incident had, after all, been an unusual and isolated case. In no time at all the matter was forgotten.

The Chemical Bullet Strikes Again

Four years later and three thousand miles away, a medical mystery occurred. On July 16, 1982, Dr. J. William Langston, a San Jose, California, neurologist, was confronted with a patient whose condition befuddled him utterly. "What I saw when I went in the patient's room was remarkable," Langston said later. "I had never seen anything like it before in my life."

The patient was George, a man in his forties who had been normal until a week before. But now he was stiffly frozen into an awkward position, unable to speak, his limbs occasionally jerking spasmodically. At first, Langston could not be certain of George's mental condition. But when George succeeded in moving his eyes according to directions, Langston realized that mentally the patient was fine.

Dr. Langston tried putting a pencil into George's hand and held a pad of paper for him to write on. "I can't move right," George managed to scrawl. "I know what I want to do; it just won't come out right. I don't know what's happening to me."[4]

Within a few days George's girlfriend, Juanita, was stricken with similar symptoms. And within a week an associate of Langston's learned of two brothers fifty miles away who were suffering the same problems.

A Medical Mystery

It seemed clear to Langston that the patients were all victims of a highly advanced form of Parkinson's disease, but the diagnosis made no sense to him. The patients were too young, and the symptoms had come on too suddenly.

Then Dr. Langston learned that all four patients were heroin abusers. It was the only link between them, and Langston was certain it had to be the key. Somehow, he believed, they had taken a toxic substance that had caused these terrible results. He immediately called a news conference to warn addicts in the area that a dangerous substance, easily substituted or mistaken for heroin, was circulating in the local drug culture.

The next day he got a call from a public health nurse who knew of another case of a paralyzed drug abuser. A young woman, Connie, twenty-six years old, had used drugs intravenously for the first time that summer. After injecting drugs on a few different occasions, Connie had become paralyzed. She could not walk, talk, or even move her arms enough to feed herself. She had been in that condition for weeks and showed no sign of improvement.

Within three weeks of the day he first saw George, Dr. Langston had a total of seven such patients. All had been heroin users; all suffered from what seemed to be an advanced case of Parkinson's disease. There was no hope of recovery for any of them.

The substance that had caused this disaster had not yet been identified. Although Dr. Langston had managed to obtain an actual sample, and it had been analyzed by his laboratory and by law-enforcement-agency laboratories, the substance remained unknown.

A Clue from the Past

Then someone remembered a medical journal article about the relationship between a toxic chemical and Parkinson's disease. The article was the story of Barry Kidston. As Dr. Langston reviewed the research done four years earlier he realized that MPTP was a possible byproduct of the process Barry had used to manufacture MPPP. Chemical analysis of the drugs Langston's patients had taken showed that MPTP was present. The connection had been made.

The discovery that a condition exactly like Parkinson's disease could be chemically induced was an important one for medical researchers. It meant they could produce the disease in animals similar to man, such as monkeys, and study the effectiveness of various types of treatment. For the tens of thousands of Americans who suffer from true Parkinson's disease, this was good news, indeed.

The Tragedy of Parkinson's Disease

For Dr. Langston's seven patients, however, there was no good news. Four had deteriorated so seriously that without constant care and regular doses of L-dopa, they would die. In Connie's case, her feet became so gnarled that she required surgery just to stand.

Although all seven responded to L-dopa, which artificially replaces the brain's supply of dopamine, the effects are temporary. The drug must be taken every two to three hours just to give the patient the ability to walk and eat. In cases this advanced, the Parkinson's victims still must spend hours frozen in their own immobilized bodies. Some of the patients are barely able to talk, even with the medication. L-dopa also has unpleasant side effects, including uncontrollable muscle movement and weight loss. And, over time, its effectiveness diminishes.

"A couple of these patients are now completely withered," says Dr. Langston. "One looks like an eighty-year-old woman."

Because Parkinson's disease is caused by the death of specific brain cells, it has no cure. "Once brain cells are gone the body can never replace them," says Dr. Langston. "There are some experiments dealing with that now, but it's tough. And her [Connie's] future is a difficult one. Connie knows this. As I say, she's a very courageous young lady but the medications lose their effectiveness with time and it's a very very difficult thing to deal with."

More Cases May Emerge

Even more frightening is the possibility that Connie and the other six patients may represent the beginning of a more widespread problem. The symptoms of Parkinson's disease are not outwardly apparent until some 80 percent of the substantia nigra has been destroyed. Two or three doses were enough to cause that level of damage in these seven patients, but Langston and others have estimated that as many as five hundred people may have been exposed to MPTP from the same contaminated batch of drugs. The initial theory was that the disease might progress more slowly in some of those people. Within five to ten years, it was believed, many of them could eventually become ill enough to require treatment. "The people who used this stuff," says Langston, "are walking time bombs."

By 1985, the theory seemed to be proving itself, as about twenty young people who had been exposed to MPTP two or three years earlier began to develop symptoms suggestive of early stages of Parkinson's disease.[5]

And although the exposure to MPTP and development of symptoms like Parkinson's was still unusual, it was occurring in other places. In 1983, in Canada, a twenty-five-year-old man developed the symptoms. He had been manufacturing an analogue of MPPP for some time and snorting it regularly. But eventually he also made an error in the process, unknowingly creating MPTP.

He snorted the toxic powder regularly over a period of seven days before finally falling ill, as his dopamine-producing brain cells were irreversibly destroyed. Because the patient seemed too young to have developed Parkinson's disease, he suffered the paralytic symptoms of the condition for a full year before a correct diagnosis was made. During that time he was kept in the mental ward of a state hospital.

Eventually he was given L-dopa, and like the other young patients before him, he responded well to the medicine. But the illness had not ended his craving for drugs. He began to abuse the L-dopa, taking excessive amounts in order to produce hallucinations. Finally, in a bizarre accident, he fell into the ocean and drowned.[6]

Perhaps one of the most surprising aspects of the MPPP/MPTP story is that the connection between use of the toxic substance and development of Parkinson's disease was ever discovered at all. "People think the medical world works like 'Quincy,' " says Dr. Darryl Inaba, recalling a once-popular TV show. On "Quincy," actor Jack Klugman played a coroner. Each week he investigated the microscopic clues he found on the bodies of murdered victims and then brilliantly deduced the identity of the killer. "It's not like that in real life," says Inaba, a pharmacologist with San Francisco's Haight-Ashbury Free Medical Clinics.[7]

But Langston's work, Inaba adds, is an exception. "MPTP was a masterpiece of scientific, medical investigation. Langston is the Quincy of our time. There are probably a lot of similar situations we haven't become aware of." The possibility that illicit synthetics may be a direct link to other illnesses is a real and frightening prospect.

"For a chemical to actually burn out or destroy a part of the brain is an extraordinarily rare event," says Dr. Gary Henderson, a California scientist who is an expert on the illicit synthetics.[8] "It can happen. In making drugs without supervision you always have the danger of overdose. Or, you have contaminants which could be toxic. The probability of something devastating happening like this parkinsonism is quite rare. But the consequences are disastrous. And that's the problem."

3
Fentanyl

William is addicted to narcotics. "The last heroin I bought," he says, "I bought from a twelve-year-old on a bicycle."[1] That was a while ago, because William is trying to give up drugs completely. He's frightened by the fact that the drug he's purchased may not be heroin at all but an analogue of the anesthetic drug fentanyl.

"In Baltimore," he says, "we've gotten a sample of some really hot drugs, and evidently it has turned out to be these designer drugs. There have been quite a few overdoses. I personally have not had any physical problems, but I know one dose could do it."

Most addicts have a hard time admitting the fact that their drug habits are life-threatening. Many also refuse to recognize that there's no way to be certain just what drug they're taking.

"I've talked to people who insist they have a 'righteous dealer,' " says Dr. Henderson. "Then we test the sample, and it turns out to be a fentanyl analogue. They can't believe it. There's no way you can tell by looking, tasting, smelling, or even using a drug, because the action of any drug can be perfectly mimicked by another."

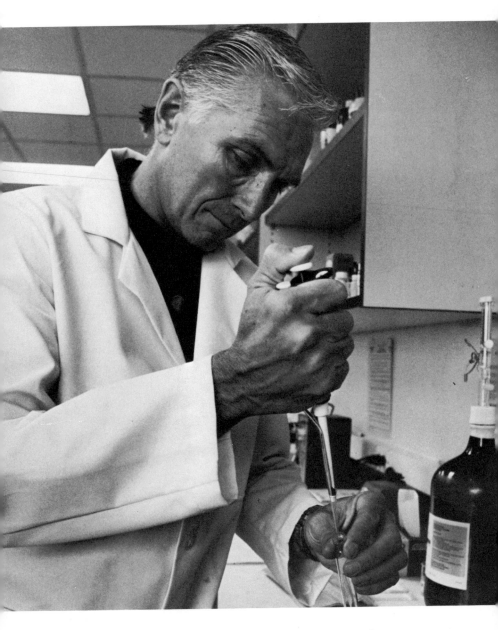

*Dr. Gary Henderson, a California scientist and
expert on illicit synthetics such as fentanyl*

This is particularly true in the case of heroin and the fentanyl analogues. Although the fentanyls have a completely different chemical structure from true narcotics, the effects are virtually the same. Users who inject or snort the analogues experience the same initial rush, or sudden feeling of euphoria, that they seek when using heroin.

The analogues also produce a painkilling effect and general slowing of body functions. This includes a reduced rate of breathing—so reduced it can be deadly. Just a few extra tiny crystals of a potent fentanyl analogue are enough to stop the natural breathing reflex and cause death. When true fentanyl is used in a surgical situation, the patient's breathing is carefully monitored and special equipment to assist with breathing is kept at hand. These safeguards are not available to those who use designer drugs.

The fentanyl analogues can also cause death by means other than respiratory depression. The medical reasons for all the overdose deaths are not fully understood. But in some cases, death comes on so quickly that addicts are found with needles still protruding from their veins.

Fentanyl Analogues

The potential number of fentanyl analogues is nearly infinite. Two widely available versions have been 3-methylfentanyl and alpha-methylfentanyl, but at least two hundred other illicit fentanyl analogues are known. Some have been created for legitimate research purposes; others have appeared first in the illicit market.[2]

Alpha-methylfentanyl and 3-methylfentanyl are both many times stronger than heroin or morphine. They are so potent that they must be measured in tiny units called *micrograms.* To understand how small these amounts are, think of a postage stamp. One postage stamp weighs 60,000 micrograms.

A few grains of alpha-methylfentanyl could cause death. However, 3-methylfentanyl is even more powerful. Any amount larger than a single salt crystal could prove deadly. The slightest mistake the chemist makes in measuring out an illicit preparation can be fatal to the unwary user.

The Fentanyl Masquerade

Many of those who use the fentanyl analogues have no idea of the risk. Most believe they are taking heroin. During the early 1980s, the fentanyls gained a reputation as a desirable drug of abuse and were actively sought and openly sold on the street. But as the dangers of designer drugs became apparent, users shunned them. In response, dealers began marketing them as heroin.

The masquerade is possible because the fentanyl analogues are just as addictive as other narcotics, and their appearance and effects are essentially the same. The illicit fentanyls even look like heroin. They are generally seen in powder form.

The powder may be colored differently, according to the guise under which the dealer intends to sell the drug —it ranges from as white as pure heroin or China White to as brown as Mexican Brown. The powder the buyer sees is not actually the drug itself, but the cane sugar or milk sugar with which it has been cut. It is impossible to actually see the amount of fentanyl in any given "dose."

Most users inject the fentanyl analogues, but they can also snort or smoke them. However the drug is taken, it has the potential to be deadly.

Fentanyl in the Brain

Like other narcotics, the fentanyl analogues interact with a specific group of nerve cells in the brain. These nerves are known as opiate receptor sites. Their existence was discovered in 1973.

As it is understood now, a specific group of naturally occurring chemicals is drawn to opiate receptor sites in the brain. These chemicals, called endorphins, represent one category of neurotransmitters, chemicals that carry messages between the brain's nerve cells. When a balanced supply of endorphins reaches the opiate receptor sites, it produces a calming effect.

A narcotic entering the brain takes over the role of the endorphins. Initially it is present in large amounts. It overwhelms the opiate receptor sites, and the user experiences euphoria.

Meanwhile the body, perceiving its own production of endorphins to be excessive, shuts down production. As the narcotic dissipates and the body's own endorphins are no longer present, other neurotransmitters begin to dominate the activity. Because they lack the soothing qualities of the endorphins, tension builds. Yet the natural means of counteracting these stresses remain disabled.[3]

The result is that a user may quickly become addicted, requiring an ongoing supply of the drug, not to experience euphoria, but to avoid feeling terribly sick. If the drug is discontinued, the result is the hellish nightmare of withdrawal. The user experiences a range of agonies including intestinal cramps, involuntary muscle spasms, vomiting, diarrhea, sweats, and a variety of other tormenting symptoms. The muscle contractions that cause involuntary movements of the legs may have given rise to the expression "kick the habit." It is fear of the withdrawal experience that prevents many users from trying to give up their drug use.

"People talk about the creepy crawlies and wanting to jump out of their skin," says one drug counselor. "The hard part is, they know that if they take just a little bit of the drug their discomforts will all go away."[4]

Withdrawal is most torturous for an initial twenty-four-to-seventy-two-hour period, but strong cravings for the drug may appear even months later. Other distressing symptoms, such as serious depression, may also persist for long periods of time.

Because the fentanyl analogues interact with the opiate receptor sites in the same way as heroin or other narcotics, addicts develop a cross dependence. If a particular narcotic is unavailable, any other will fulfill the craving.

Tolerance

Whichever narcotic the drug abuser chooses to use, over time he or she will develop a physical tolerance for the presence of narcotics. As tolerance develops, it becomes necessary to take larger and larger doses in order to avoid feeling sick. The euphoria the drug once produced occurs no more. Instead, the drug serves only to produce a state of being that the user now perceives as "normal."

This condition, in which the user craves the drug constantly and requires it in order to avoid the excruciating symptoms of withdrawal, is known as addiction. Because of their regular and heavy use, addicts may sometimes develop an astonishing tolerance for the drugs they abuse. In some cases, they have been found to have fifty times more fentanyl in their system than was found in the system of victims presumed to have died by overdose.

The danger of narcotics overdose, therefore, is particularly great for the novice user or curious individual who just wants to try it once or twice. Strength of drugs purchased on the street is unpredictable and unreliable. An addict's routine dose can easily prove fatal for the first-time or occasional user.

Who Uses Fentanyl Analogues?

The fentanyls seem to be most widely used among long-time addicts. But the analogues have also been known to fall into the hands of other users. In Fresno, California, during the height of fentanyl's availability in 1984, a nineteen-year-old girl was housesitting for some friends. While she was there she came across a stash of drugs. She decided to try snorting some white powder she found. She did not know that the powder was fentanyl that had not yet been cut into individual doses.

"She probably thought it was cocaine," says a Drug Enforcement Administration (DEA) agent familiar with the case. "But what she snorted was a load of dynamite."[5] Her body was found the next morning when the home-owners returned. The investigation prompted by her death, as well as several other deaths tied to the same batch of fentanyl, ultimately resulted in the closing of a major fentanyl analogue lab in Los Angeles.

Despite such incidents, young people sometimes knowingly use the drug. In some areas teenagers smoke a mixture of fentanyl analogues and cocaine. Others use the analogues as a way of coming down from cocaine.

The Demand for Synthetic Heroin

There was a period during the mid-1980s when some drug users, having heard of the strong effects of the new synthetics, were specifically asking for those drugs on the street. They seemed unconcerned about the dangers of death by overdose. "A true full-blown drug addict would follow a morgue wagon to its origin of overdose to obtain that substance," observed William, himself a longtime addict.

The threat of being permanently disabled may have been more frightening. As publicity concerning the outbreak of Parkinson's disease in San Jose spread, demand for the new "synthetic heroin" dropped off for a couple of years. But by early 1988, it was reappearing.

Still, it is impossible to know how many drug abusers are using fentanyl at any given time. Many of them believe they are taking heroin, since cost, appearance, and

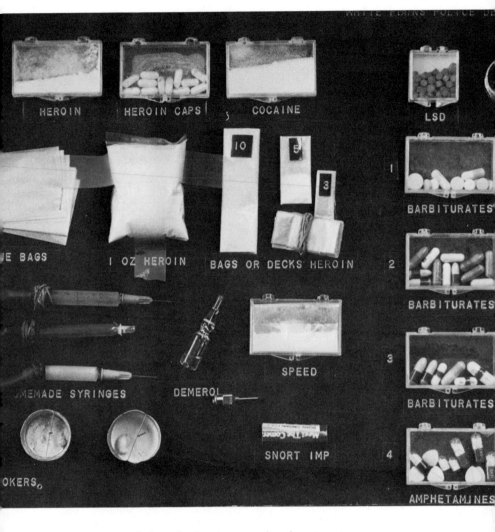

A drug display from a police department shows various narcotics. Drug users often cannot tell the difference between actual heroin (pictured in the middle of the display) and fentanyl analogues because they look exactly alike.

effects of the drugs are virtually identical. Some 20 percent of California's addicts are estimated to have been using fentanyl analogues during 1984 and 1985, but that figure is little more than a guess.[6]

Hazards

The greatest danger of use of any of the fentanyl analogues is death by overdose. The minute quantities that constitute a survivable dose, and the haphazard way in which the drug is illicitly manufactured and distributed, are a potentially fatal combination.

Use of any of these synthetics also carries all the well-known dangers of possession or use of heroin and other narcotics. The probability of addiction is extremely high. The dangers of transmission of certain diseases, such as hepatitis, through use of shared or contaminated needles are well documented.

The emergence of AIDS has created another serious risk for drug users. Sharing of needles among carriers of the AIDS virus has been shown to be a primary means of transmission of this fatal disease.

Possession of illicit drugs is illegal, and the possibility of going to jail must also be counted as a primary hazard. Possession of even trace amounts of illicit narcotics carries maximum sentences of up to fifteen years in prison. For those who choose to use drugs, prison easily becomes part of the pattern. A Department of Justice study has shown that up to 75 percent of males involved in crimes use illicit drugs. The figures for females are not yet fully compiled, but early indications are that the percentage of women who commit crimes after using drugs is even higher.[7]

History

Fentanyl was first developed in Europe and introduced in this country in 1972 under the trade name Sublimaze.

Today it is used in about 70 percent of all surgeries in America. It is considered an ideal surgical drug because it produces a short-term anesthesia. In fact, the effects of fentanyl are so brief that the drug was believed to have little potential for abuse.[8]

That situation changed with the development of the first illicit fentanyl analogue, alpha-methylfentanyl, around 1979. The hazardous potential of this powerful new analogue became apparent in 1980 when mysterious overdose cases began to appear.

As Dr. Henderson recalls, "We found that fentanyl, or derivatives of fentanyl, were being made, sold, and used as heroin substitutes here in California. There were overdose deaths, but they could find no drug at all in the body. The reason they couldn't find any drug was because fentanyl cannot be detected by conventional methods."[9]

While California coroners tried to determine the cause of death in a number of seemingly unrelated incidents, there were some other curious occurrences. Several self-described addicts applied for admission to methadone treatment facilities in Contra Costa County. They were refused when the results of their urine tests showed no trace of heroin.[10]

Initially, officials were confused. Why would anyone falsely claim a serious heroin habit? It soon became apparent that the addicts, who believed they had been using heroin, had actually been taking a new fentanyl analogue.

Between 1980, when the fentanyl analogues first surfaced, and the summer of 1987, over one hundred overdose deaths were tied to fentanyl analogues. This figure may well be low. The tiny amounts in which fentanyl is used, and at which it can be lethal, make it extremely difficult to detect in body fluids. Because some fentanyl overdose deaths are undoubtedly often listed instead as deaths by "unknown cause," there is no way to know exactly how many drug users have been killed by fentanyl analogues.

4
Methamphetamine

When Cindy was fourteen years old she injected methamphetamine for the first time. She had been snorting the
drug regularly for four months when a friend offered to
show her how to shoot it. "It's something I thought I'd
never do," she recalls. "I used to see people shooting and
I'd always say, if I ever get as bad as that, I'll quit."

Instead, Cindy found she couldn't quit. Her need and
tolerance for the drug were increasing tremendously. "It
got so I'd shoot four or five times a day," she says. "Once
I stayed up for nine days straight. After a while I started
hallucinating. And I thought I was covered with tweak
bugs. I could *see* them on my skin. And I'd scratch and take
showers but they'd still be there."

What Is Methamphetamine?

The drug Cindy was using, *methamphetamine,* is a white
powder often referred to as "poor man's cocaine" because,
like cocaine, it is a nervous system stimulant. It was once
a legal drug prescribed for specific medical problems, but

its hazards have been found to outweigh its medical value.

On the street methamphetamine goes under such names as crank, speed, gofast, and crystal meth. A potent stimulant, it is actually an analogue of the first amphetamine developed, a drug most commonly known by its trade name, Benzedrine. Although amphetamine and its variations have been widely abused for years, use of illicitly manufactured methamphetamine is becoming increasingly widespread.

In the late 1970s and early 1980s, when cocaine was hard to obtain and therefore extremely expensive, methamphetamine was a cheaper way to experience a similar effect. In recent years, however, the two drugs have often cost about the same.

Methamphetamine can be snorted, injected, or even stirred into a hot drink such as coffee. Because its effects are more long-lasting than those of cocaine and because it is readily obtainable, methamphetamine use has been spreading.

The Methamphetamine Experience

The attraction of methamphetamine lies in the feeling of happiness and well-being it promotes the first few times it is used. "It was just the intense wire," says Bill, who began using methamphetamine when he was fourteen. "You'd be glad to be wherever you were. You could be alone in a dark room and you'd be having fun."

The initial feeling of euphoria lasts from two to four hours, depending on the amount and quality of drug taken. The feeling of being wired—alert, excitable, unable to sleep or eat—lasts six to eight hours more. During this second phase many users stay busy, performing some task that seems productive at the time. They strongly feel that the drug enhances their creativity, insight, and ability to carry out tasks. Bill, for instance, says that when using

methamphetamine he would often do his homework. But in the morning he usually found that whatever he had written was unreadable or made little sense.

Gradually the euphoria wears off and the drug user is left feeling restless and edgy. The user feels wired or "tweaked."

During this phase, sleep is impossible, however tired the user may be. He or she may be hungry, but is unable to eat. "Even if you do try to eat something," says one user, "it's just like putting a sponge down your throat."

People who feel wired are likely to be talkative, animated, and active. But they may also experience strong feelings of apprehension and nervousness—paranoia. They have a constant urge to look out the window, watching who's coming and going, and an uncontrollable fear that parents or police may walk in at any moment, however unlikely that may be.

As the effects of the drug wear off, the user experiences a sense of profound depression. "You feel so emotional," says Cindy. "The littlest thing would make me cry. And I'd swear I'd never do crank again."

But she did, again and again.

Reaching for Euphoria

The "lie" of methamphetamine—that euphoria is just a snort away—draws users to try it again and again. The first time or two it's used, methamphetamine gives the

Police empty drying trays of suspected methamphetamine into evidence bags after raiding a doctor's office. The medical doctor was suspected of manufacturing and selling the drugs from a laboratory set up in his basement.

user a profound sense of joy and well-being. "Crank is more intense, more of a high," says Mark, a nineteen-year-old recovering methamphetamine addict. "It's very different from speed. Speed [amphetamine] just makes you feel awake. Crank is more mental."

Mark started using drugs heavily when he was seventeen. And although he became enamored of crank almost immediately, he was also quick to recognize another of its drawbacks. "The first wire was really great," he recalls. "I was always trying to recapture the way it was that time, but I never could. You can never get back to it."

One of the great dangers of methamphetamine is that every user wants to regain that initial level of euphoria. This means taking the drug more frequently, in larger doses, moving up from snorting to injecting, trying to experience once more that state of bliss that remains tantalizingly out of reach.

The desire to use methamphetamine, to experience the feeling of happiness it once brought, is frighteningly powerful. Those who frequently inject it may have difficulty in finding a vein. They may inject the drug directly into the neck, between the toes, or under the tongue.

These desperate actions continue even though the drug no longer provides the type of high the user is seeking and anticipating. "It got to where it wasn't fun," Cindy recalls. "I had to have it just to function. After a while I had to have a lot of it just to get a little bit high."

In addition, Cindy found the drug was having other negative effects. The "tweak bugs" she imagined were crawling all over her body are a common side effect of methamphetamine. She also developed an acnelike rash known among users as speed bumps. Her skin itched, she found it hard to eat normally, and she felt nervous and frightened all the time.

In addition to the unpleasant physical effects of the drug, injecting methamphetamine carries the dangers of hepatitis or AIDS transmission through unclean needles.

The urge to take the drug makes the user oblivious to these or other hazards. "I started breaking into people's houses to take things to sell for drug money," says Dale, a classmate of Cindy's. Even when he was caught, he did not want to give up the drug.

Methamphetamine
and Addiction

Regular users find it difficult to abandon the drug, despite unpleasant experiences such as frightening hallucinations or uncomfortable physical sensations. Their high is simply too enticing.

"I believe that the drive to take crank is five times stronger than for heroin," says one drug counselor, who has worked with hundreds of methamphetamine abusers. "Kids don't usually stop until they've gotten into big trouble. They think the drug is safe because it's psychologically rather than physically addicting. They think they can handle it. When they experience ill effects, they blame them not on the crank, but on the cutter. They tend to think they just got a bad batch, even if it happens again and again."

Not every crank user becomes addicted or gets hooked as quickly as Cindy did, but many do find themselves craving it more than any other drug. "I loved it because I thought I could accomplish anything," says Bill, sixteen. "I could talk to people easily, do homework, do all the things that make my parents proud of me. I'd get wired and do my chores, clean my room, everything."

Unlike Cindy, Bill never progressed to injecting. But the effects of crank quickly made it his drug of choice.

Methamphetamine
in the Brain

The key to the drug's powerful attraction lies in the way it acts on specific cells in the brain. Some types of drugs,

(45)

such as heroin or morphine, act to block pain from our awareness, creating a somewhat numbed sense of well-being; methamphetamine, on the other hand, actually stimulates the brain to experience pleasure.

This occurs because methamphetamine interferes with the production of the neurotransmitter dopamine. Higher levels of dopamine increase feelings of well-being and happiness. When levels of dopamine are low, some depression may set in. But the overall balance is such that people remain emotionally stable.

Recent studies, including one done at the University of Chicago, have shown that methamphetamine raises the level of dopamine far beyond normal levels.[1] This results in a state of excited euphoria.

As the effects of the drug wear off, the mood changes completely. The level of dopamine drops dramatically. Instead of being overwhelmed by its presence, the neurons now have an inadequate supply of the dopamine they need to maintain normal feelings of well-being. The user becomes increasingly depressed. "When I was on the drug I wanted to be more and more wired," says Bill. "When I came down it was totally different. I'd get sick every time. I'd eat and throw up. I'd wish I'd never taken any crank."

As the level of drug use increases, the degree of depression that the user experiences as part of the cycle of use may become more profound and begin to affect other aspects of life.

"After a while," says Bill, "I didn't like myself anymore. I was always depressed. I was failing school. I was cutting classes. I realized that crank was getting me nowhere. It's all a lie."

Methamphetamine
and Violence

Methamphetamine use can lead to violence. Tom Streed is a detective with the Homicide Division of the San

Diego County Sheriff's Department. He also holds a Ph.D. in criminal psychology. In recent years he has documented the violence that sometimes accompanies methamphetamine use. "We've found that methamphetamine users have tremendous mood swings," Streed says.[2] "There is a tremendous factor of unpredictability. They can erupt with very little or no provocation. Their personality constantly changes. It ebbs and flows."

One factor that differentiates the methamphetamine experience from that of some other drugs, Streed explains, is that occasional use results in an illusional state of mind, rather than the delusional condition some other drugs cause. To explain the difference, he cites one case in which a group of people, high on methamphetamine, were driving down the highway. Suddenly the driver slammed on his brakes, jumped out of the car, ran to the vehicle behind him, and threatened the man with a gun. The driver had the strong illusion that the man in the car behind him had been a threat.

But when he returned to his own car, the people with him said there hadn't been a problem: "It's just the crank." He realized they were right. In other words, even while under the influence of the drug, he recognized that his visions and fears were the result of having taken methamphetamine.

In the case of a delusional state, such as that brought on by certain hallucinogenic drugs, it is impossible to convince the person that visions, no matter how bizarre, are not real.[3]

With frequent methamphetamine or amphetamine use, the drug begins to control all perception, and the user experiences amphetamine psychosis. At this point, all awareness of reality is lost.

Even occasional methamphetamine use can lead to violence. In one case, a twenty-year-old man argued with a friend over a fifty-dollar drug purchase. The young man exploded into anger and beat his friend into unconsciousness with an aluminum baseball bat. Then he went to another room for a handgun, returned, and shot his victim four times.

To dispose of the body, the murderer drove miles away into an area of isolated foothills and dumped it along a dirt road. But in one of the acts of seeming irrationality that accompany such incidents, he also dumped bags of trash from his own home, leaving police a direct trail. The man was easily apprehended and readily convicted of the crime.

Detective Streed has seen many cases in which the state of mind brought on by methamphetamine played a distinct role. Methamphetamine use can cause extreme panic and an exaggerated reaction to almost any event. "These murders are generally of a spontaneous nature as the result of an emotional outburst," Streed says. "They are carried out with a mixture of cunning and nonsensical behavior. When we catch these people the explanations they give are almost childlike."

The Extent of Methamphetamine Use

Methamphetamine has long been heavily used in urban centers such as Philadelphia, San Diego, and San Francisco, and is also prevalent in Dallas, New Orleans, Phoenix, Denver, and Sacramento.[4] In 1985, one survey showed that 23 percent of young people aged twelve to twenty-five had tried stimulants at least once. That's nearly seven million people.[5]

Both Cindy and Bill attended treatment programs when their parents learned of their drug problem. Although the two teenagers are now free of drugs, they are not free of the urge to use crank again. "I don't know what I'd do if I got in a situation where it was available," Cindy admits. "It would be hard."

It is a problem Cindy will almost certainly have to confront. Of all the illicit synthetics, methamphetamine is the most readily available.

Methamphetamines, along with marijuana, various firearms, and laboratory equipment, confiscated by police during a drug raid

Although methamphetamine seems to have become a drug of the eighties, there is nothing new about it. The first amphetamine was synthesized in 1887. But the drug had no particular medical use until 1927, when it was used in asthma treatment.[6] It was believed to be useful for enlarging the bronchial and nasal passages.

Other versions, or analogues, of amphetamine, were also being developed, including methamphetamine, which was first synthesized in 1919. By 1971, fifteen pharmaceutical companies were marketing thirty-one amphetamine preparations for medicinal use.

(Amphetamine was first marketed for medicinal use in 1932 under the trade name Benzedrine. It was widely prescribed for increased energy and wakefulness. During World War II amphetamines were routinely issued to soldiers of several different nations.

After a few years, an odd aspect of amphetamines came to light. Despite the fact that they tend to make adults feel more active and energetic, they have a calming effect on children suffering from hyperactivity.[7] They have also been prescribed for treatment of narcolepsy, a disorder that causes the affected person to fall asleep spontaneously at inopportune and unexpected moments. Amphetamines have also been used, rather casually, as an aid to weight loss.

Their potential for abuse was, however, soon recognized. Abuse of amphetamines, then known as "pep pills," was reported as early as 1940.[8]

For years, abusers obtained amphetamines illicitly through doctors' offices, pharmaceutical companies, or other sources. Thus, the drugs used, although illegally obtained, were produced by legitimate pharmaceutical houses. But in 1965 new drug laws were passed, making it far more difficult to procure the drugs. That step was highly effective, so much so that it was during the 1960s that the first illicit amphetamine and methamphetamine labs began to appear. Because of the sharp curtailment in medical use of the drug and the tight restrictions, virtually all the methamphetamine on the street today has been made in underground labs.

5
Ecstasy

Orion is twenty years old. He dropped out of school in his early teens and left home to travel on his own. Along the way he has experimented with many different drugs. His experiences have led him to believe that drugs offer only false promises and real dangers. Even so, he readily admits there is one drug that still tempts him.

"I've done other things already and I know what they're like," he explains. "I don't want to get too involved. I would do MDMA again, but it would have to be a while. That's the only one I could really say I'd take."

What Is MDMA?

The drug Orion would try again is MDMA (3-4-methylenedioxymethamphetamine), also known as Ecstasy, XTC, Adam, or M-methyl. MDMA is chemically similar to both methamphetamine and another drug, MDA (3, 4-methylenedioxyamphetamine). from which it was derived. A German pharmaceutical company developed MDMA in 1914, with the idea of selling it as a dietary aid.

But early tests quickly showed that the drug had too many negative effects. It occasionally caused nausea, and no one would want to take a medicine that would cause vomiting. So MDMA was never marketed. The formula seems to have languished, unnoticed, for decades.

Ecstasy is sold as a pill or a powder in capsules to be taken orally. Sometimes the powder is removed and snorted. But no guarantee exists that those capsules actually do contain MDMA. Other drugs, such as MDA or PCP, may be substituted. Sometimes the expensive capsules, which can cost from eight to forty dollars, contain nothing but sugar. According to one researcher, "Someone who thinks she is buying MDMA might be getting just about anything masquerading as Ecstasy. There is absolutely no such thing as quality control on the street. The range of misrepresentation is staggering. Using these drugs outside a doctor's office is like playing Russian roulette."[1]

These four different drugs have similar chemical structures.

The MDMA Experience

Even when the drug *is* MDMA, individual reactions vary widely. Generally the experience progresses in three phases. About thirty minutes after taking the drug there is a period of slight disorientation and distress. This may include chills, sweating, nausea, and uncontrollable rapid eye movements called nystagmus. In some cases, the experience never progresses beyond this phase. For those users, Ecstasy means a nightmare of throwing up and painful dry heaves.

In most cases, a few moments of slight discomfort are followed by a period of "happy sociability" that can last from two to four hours. "It's very beautiful and can show a person a lot, like psychedelics," says Orion. "It shows people avenues of their self that they never even thought of before. Where psychedelics open the mind, MDMA opens the heart. And you get into stuff like universal love.

"It's like, you get this slow steady rush of, everything's beautiful. You want to hold on to your friends. It's not a sexual thing. It's sort of a friendship kind of love." MDMA is, in fact, often known as the "hug drug" because it promotes feelings of warmth and friendship without physical intimacy. MDA is more likely to be taken by those seeking to enhance sexual experience.

"You really get into grabbing with MDMA," says Orion. "You get into chewing too. A lot of people, when they're on it, they chew on carrots. To an outsider it could look pretty strange. You come down and feel great for weeks, if it's pure. Not if it's impure, like a lot of the stuff is, because the chemists just want to make it and make money off it. The lab work can be sloppy and you don't feel the same way."

Some MDMA users hallucinate. And as with methamphetamine, they eventually crash. Feelings of anxiety, confusion, and depression usually last about twenty-four hours, but may hang on for weeks.

Flasks containing liquid MDMA in
an illicit drug lab found by police

MDMA and Addiction

MDMA users are less likely to become addicted than users of drugs such as synthetic heroin or even methamphetamine. The reason for this, although not fully understood, may be related to the way MDMA affects the brain chemicals. Another factor is that, with regular use, the euphoric aspect of the experience diminishes though the negative effects remain, sometimes becoming even more intensified.

"If someone takes a drug and it makes them throw up right away, they're not going to take it again," says Dr. Ronald Siegel, a psychopharmacologist at the UCLA School of Medicine's Department of Psychiatry. "Why? It didn't deliver the ecstasy it promised. It made them feel sick. So they didn't go back to it."[2]

MDMA in the Brain

MDMA and MDA both upset the normal balance of the important neurotransmitters dopamine and serotonin. MDMA and MDA stimulate dopamine production, resulting in a range of states from euphoria to psychosis. But as the drug wears off, the body cannot maintain the high dopamine level, and a scarcity of that substance follows. The state of mind changes to depression.

Artificial manipulation of serotonin levels affects sleep patterns, sexual activity, aggression, mood, and pain sensitivity.

A study conducted at the University of Chicago has shown that permanent brain damage may result from high levels of MDA and MDMA use.

Scientists who injected monkeys and rats with MDA found that even a single use of the substance could destroy neurons that accept the messages carried by serotonin. Regular use of MDMA can cause similar damage at even lower doses.[3]

Death by MDMA

MDMA use has one other potential effect, one that is immediate and permanent: death. The extent of the risk is not fully known, but documented cases exist. In Dallas County, Texas, an area where Ecstasy has been extremely popular, five deaths were tied to MDMA and a similar synthetic, MDEA, over a nine-month period in 1985 and 1986.[4]

In three of the deaths, use of MDMA or MDEA apparently aggravated existing health conditions. In one case, a thirty-two-year-old asthmatic died after taking MDMA. In the two other cases, young men died of heart attacks after taking MDEA, an MDMA analogue that they believed to be MDMA. Both men had preexisting heart conditions of which they had been unaware.

The fourth case illustrated the effects of MDMA on

judgment. A twenty-two-year-old man took MDMA, then climbed an electric utility tower. He was electrocuted and fell to his death.

The fifth death was that of an eighteen-year-old woman. She took two hits of MDMA, about 150 milligrams, along with some alcoholic drinks over a period of an hour to ninety minutes. She then collapsed and died. Of this particular group of deaths, hers was the only one apparently caused solely by taking MDMA.

How exactly did the drug kill her? Again, researchers simply don't know. According to Dr. Darryl Inaba, "Two to three percent of people will have a major toxic episode just from one exposure to a drug."

The Extent of MDMA Use

MDMA began to appear on the street in the 1970s. But it was just one of many illicit drugs, and it attracted little special attention. Its use was so sparse that even though DEA officials were aware of its existence no effort was made to add it to the roster of banned drugs.

All that changed in the early 1980s. As with so many things in America, MDMA profited mightily from a good dose of public relations. The drug was renamed Ecstasy, it was packaged along with trendy-sounding instructions, and it was made available on college campuses. Because Ecstasy was perfectly legal, it was sold openly in bars and discotheques frequented by students. In some of those places, customers reportedly could charge their drug purchases to their credit cards.

Since 1978 over 70,000 dosage units of MDMA have been submitted to DEA officials for analysis. It has also been reported that in 1985 a single individual in Dallas was distributing as many as 30,000 dosage units per month.[5] Just a few years earlier the entire annual consumption of MDMA had been estimated at around 10,000 dosage units.[6]

A New Analogue

On July 1, 1985, MDMA was officially banned. Illicit labs were closed and dealers arrested. The DEA placed MDMA in the most restricted category, along with heroin and LSD. Because MDMA had no broadly accepted medical use and showed a high potential for abuse, tight controls were deemed necessary.

Within days of the banning, a new, similar drug appeared. The new drug was a close analogue of MDMA. It was MDE (3,4-methylenedioxy-N-ethylamphetamine), called Eve on the street.

Eve reportedly had the same effects as Ecstasy. But nothing about Eve was really known—not its action in the brain, not its toxic dosage levels, not even its precise physical and psychological effects.

Yet because Eve had not been legally identified and scheduled, its use was perfectly legal. In 1985, the outlook was that, although Eve would soon be controlled, another new analogue would surely be on the scene within weeks.

The MDMA Controversy

The banning of MDMA did not take place without an uproar. It has been legally challenged by Lester Grinspoon, a Harvard research psychiatrist who would like to see the drug made available to medical researchers under strict controls. While Dr. Grinspoon won a lower court ruling, the DEA was able to retain MDMA's Schedule I listing by introducing new criteria. The final classification of this controversial drug will no doubt be made one day by the U.S. Supreme Court.

Grinspoon is one of a group of psychotherapists who feel that MDMA could be a useful medicine. The drug has seemed to help some patients talk more openly about past experiences, share feelings more freely, and recognize the hidden motives controlling their behavior. According to some doctors, moderate doses of MDMA used under strictly controlled conditions might help patients resolve their psychological problems.[7]

UCLA's Dr. Siegel says MDMA causes "nowhere near the brain damage we definitely know occurs irreversibly with alcohol." And it is still not clear whether the results of the University of Chicago study, which showed that MDA and MDMA cause brain damage, would also apply to humans, since that study was conducted solely on animals.

Other researchers have found that the psychological effects of MDMA use are also potentially harmful.[8] They believe that a severe negative impact may result from the release of strong emotions when the drug is taken outside a medically supervised situation. And as Dr. Seiden, a researcher on the effects of the drug, has said, "We are not yet exactly sure of Ecstasy's neurotoxic effects, but when very similar drugs demonstrate nerve cell death and potential disruption of key brain functions, it is likely that MDMA's consequences are equally serious."[9]

Although scientists do not fully agree on the extent of the hazards of MDMA, MDA, and related drugs, one thing is certain: using illicitly manufactured street drugs is dangerous. Dosages are unknown, contaminants are likely to be present, and the identity of the drug itself must always be suspect. Death or permanent brain damage is a steep price to pay for a few moments of ecstasy.

6
PCP

On the street it has a hundred names—angel dust, rocket fuel, HOG, and crystal, to name just a few. Under its influence people have jumped out of high-rise buildings, deliberately driven their cars into oncoming traffic, even murdered their own children.[1] The drug is PCP, short for phencyclidine. Its bizarre effects are well known. Because of those effects, in some regions the drug is considered a poison and is avoided. In others, it is highly sought.

The PCP Experience

"I used it only once," says Jeannie. "I'll never touch it again."

Jeannie was seventeen when she had her PCP experience. She was at a party and took a drag from a marijuana joint being passed around. She didn't know the joint had been dipped into PCP. "All of a sudden everything felt really far away," she says. "People talk to you, and it's like they're so far away, you can't hear them."

Jeannie knew that the people she was with sometimes

used PCP. When the strange effects began, she immediately realized their cause. PCP is often mixed with other drugs, or substituted for them, and unknowing users may find themselves in a panic as the unexpected effects take over.

"I had no sensation in my body," says Jeannie. "The sensation was there, but it was apart from me. I had the feeling that my heart was beating but my brain was dead. I felt I was dying. I wanted to tell the people with me that I was dead. To me, PCP is a death drug."

The drug does not affect everyone in the same way. "I liked to take PCP to get high," says Kevin, who used the drug regularly for several years. "One joint got four people like they were a little bit drunk. Sometimes I've seen them freak out, sweat and get scared. Mostly I felt lightheaded, giggly, but with zero energy."

Usually Kevin smoked PCP in cigarettes made with parsley or marijuana, but once he tried it in the crystal form. "There was just a little residue left in a baggie," he says. "I scraped it up and put it on my tongue, but it tasted so awful I spat it out. I thought nothing had happened."

Instead, the PCP sent Kevin into a strange mental state of which he remembers nothing. The ten hours during which he was under the drug's total influence are a complete blank, despite the fact that he was very active. Later he was told some of the things that happened. "A neighbor came over and got my kid," Kevin says. "He saw me in front of the house and knew I was in no condition to take care of him. My friend came over and I broke his nose and blacked both of his eyes. Later he asked me why I did it, and I said I didn't know. To this day I don't remember it."

How PCP Is Used

The precise effects of PCP can vary tremendously, depending on the dosage, the purity of the drug, the means by which it is taken, and the particular body chemistry of the individual user.

PCP is sometimes found as a tablet, powder, or crystal, but more recently it has been most popular in a liquid form. This liquid is an especially hazardous variation because it is far more likely to contain impurities such as cyanide, the same deadly poison used to kill prisoners in the gas chamber.

Most commonly, cigarettes of marijuana, parsley, or even tobacco are dipped into PCP and then smoked. These may be called shermans, joysticks, happy sticks, or clickers.

PCP is used in other ways too. Sometimes it is eaten with peanut butter or added to fruit juice. It can also be injected or, when in powder form, snorted. It doesn't even have to be directly ingested or smoked. PCP can be absorbed through the skin. The simple act of touching a PCP-contaminated surface can make you high.

The Effects of PCP

There is no way to predict just what the effects will be. PCP may act as a stimulant, revving up the nervous system; a depressant, producing a languid state of detachment; or a hallucinogen, causing weird visions and distorted perception.

The high associated with PCP usually peaks in fifteen to twenty minutes and may last three to five hours. It is not always pleasant. "For me there was a rush," says Jeannie, "but it was a rush of scared paranoia."

Colorful hallucinations of the type associated with LSD are rare among PCP users. More often they experience a floating sensation and a physical and emotional numbness. They may walk around, mouth hanging open, appearing to be doing everything in slow motion. Some users sit perfectly still, gazing into space, seemingly unable to move. Others may engage in extremely strange

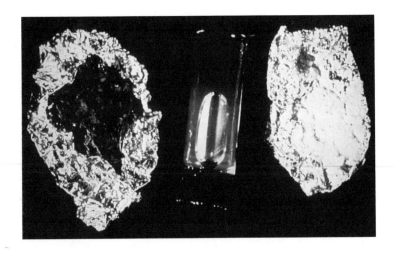

PCP in crystal, tablet, and powder forms

behavior, taking off their clothes and walking nude in public places, jumping out of windows, or violently attacking bystanders for no apparent reason.

In upper New York State, PCP use resulted in a brutal murder that typifies the odd effects of this drug. In that case, a seventeen-year-old boy was attacked by two friends who accused him of stealing some of their PCP. Under the influence of the drug they gouged out his eyes and then stabbed him to death. They were quickly apprehended by police. While in jail, one of the boys hanged himself with a sheet from his cot.[2]

Such violent episodes are not uncommon when PCP is in the picture. In San Jose, California, a city where PCP is widely used, police report that 22 percent of all murders in 1985 were PCP-related. At any given time about half the police officers on disability leave have been injured in encounters with people high on PCP.

Accidents of a more mundane nature are also routine. Because the user loses physical control and experiences distorted perception, he or she is likely to have an accident if driving. Falling, sometimes after deliberately jumping from great heights, is another cause of injury under the influence of PCP. Drowning deaths occur when PCP users try to enhance the "floating" sensation the drug produces by floating in actual water. While intoxicated on PCP they just can't swim.

The drug causes users to feel a mix of emotions that range from a sense of being all-powerful, to anxiety, to rage and depression. Because PCP does have an anesthetic effect, users feel little or no pain and often seem to have an almost superhuman strength. The result is a potential for destructive, dangerous behavior. Yet as they return to a more normal state, all memory of that behavior vanishes. Thus, PCP users often refuse to believe they have actually committed the strange acts described by their friends.

PCP produces a delusional state of mind in which the user believes that distorted perceptions, actually the creation of the drug that has been taken, are absolutely real. The normal patterns of logic and reasoning are lost, making it difficult or impossible to talk rationally with a person under the influence of PCP. LSD users can often be talked down from a bad trip; however, a friendly presence doesn't help or reassure the PCP user. In fact, the mental state the drug produces is so similar to the mental illness of schizophrenia that doctors have been known to mistake PCP users for schizophrenics. This psychosis, or detachment from reality, may last only for the period during which the drug is being used, or it may last for days or weeks.[3]

The Lure of PCP

Given all the negative effects, what is the attraction of this drug? "I started taking it because everybody else was," says Kevin. "It would be brought out at a party."

Kevin says that at first he liked the sense of detachment

and lack of caring that went with the drug. "When people talked to you, it was like they were in an echo chamber. Everything looked like it would through the bottom of a Coke bottle. And you don't care about anything. Someone could come up and cut your feet off and you just wouldn't care."

The drug's easy availability is the main reason some young people choose to use it. Others, knowing that its effects make PCP use a dangerous and risky proposition, take the drug in search of adventure.

For users like Kevin and Jeannie, the adventure isn't worth the negative feelings. "I couldn't control my *self* on PCP," Kevin says. "I couldn't control what was going on around me. That scared me. And it wasn't a good high. It wasn't a fun high."

PCP Dependence

When Kevin decided to give up PCP, he was able to do so with little difficulty. PCP is not considered a physically addictive drug, in that users who decide to discontinue its use experience virtually no withdrawal symptoms. In addition, ongoing use of PCP does not necessarily result in the need to take ever greater doses to achieve the desired effects. However, there may be a strong psychological urge to continue the experience.[4]

Those who give in to that urge are often looked down upon by other drug users. "We always considered PCP users to be dirt, pure skunge," says a young woman whose friends use other drugs. "They cared nothing for their friends or neighbors. They became heavy addicts who would do destructive things. They lost all reality."

PCP in the Brain

The means by which PCP distorts reality are not fully understood. Like many other illicit drugs that affect the brain and behavior, PCP interacts with the neurotransmitters, those chemicals that carry messages and impulses. As we have seen, changing levels of neurotransmitters can affect moods and emotions as well as muscle coordination.

Studies have shown that use of PCP has a toxic effect on certain brain activities. The result of this disturbance can be a difficulty in learning that will directly affect the user's ability to succeed in school or on the job.[5]

When PCP is used regularly, memory, perception, concentration, and judgment are all affected long after the "high" of the drug has ended.

Other Toxic Effects

PCP has other toxic effects on the body. In large doses, it impairs the disease-fighting ability of white blood cells.[6] It can be deadly when combined with barbiturates and narcotics. The PCP user who seeks routine dental care while intoxicated on PCP may be making a fatal appointment. The effects of some painkilling drugs used by a dentist or doctor become exaggerated in patients in whom PCP is present. Mixed with alcohol or tranquilizers, PCP can cause coma leading to death. Used by very young people, it may interfere with growth hormones.

PCP is extremely hazardous to young children, who seem to experience even more severe effects than adults. Children often have a toxic reaction just from being near people smoking PCP—the secondhand smoke is enough to cause them to become frozen in position, staring fixedly at some distant point.

In one recent case in California, a twenty-one-year-old woman was convicted of involuntary manslaughter after her baby died from eating a PCP-laced cigarette he had found on the floor. Such cases, in which toddlers become dangerously sick after eating PCP-soaked butts, are not unusual in areas where abuse levels are high.

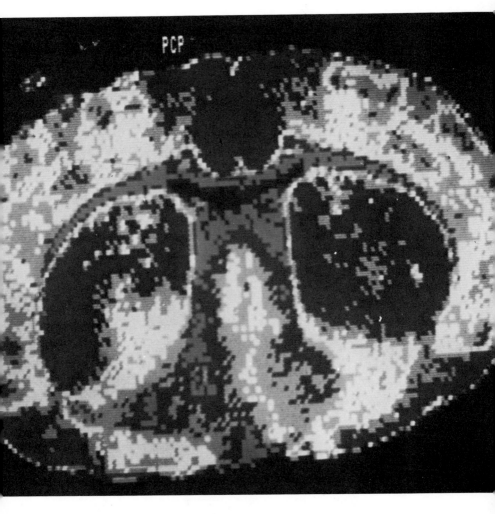

A computerized brain scan shows the effects of PCP on an animal brain. A majority of the area indicates uncontrolled brain activity similar to that seen in severe schizophrenia. There is speculation that PCP causes intense metabolic activity that may ultimately exhaust the brain.

The unborn are also at risk. PCP easily crosses from the mother into the baby, causing the fetus's heartbeat to increase irregularly, and blood pressure to rise or fall. Because the baby's undeveloped body is unable to diffuse and eliminate the drug, it stays in the baby much longer. After birth, such babies tend to be irritable and experience facial twitching and body tremors.

The Extent of PCP Use

Despite its unpredictable, often negative effects, PCP is widely used in some areas. PCP consumption is particularly widespread in the inner cities, especially among blacks and Hispanics. In Chicago, St. Louis, Detroit, Los Angeles, Washington, D.C., San Diego, and New Orleans, PCP use is extremely high.

Among high school students, use of PCP has decreased slightly over the past four years. In 1982, 6 percent of high school seniors had tried PCP at least once. By 1986, that figure had dipped to just under 5 percent.[7] Nonetheless, by the age of twenty-five, nearly five million young people have tried a hallucinogenic drug at least once. That category includes LSD, mescaline, and psilocybin, as well as PCP. Currently, PCP is the most widely used of that group of drugs.

There is also another way to measure the prevalence of a drug: by looking at the number of emergency-room visits and deaths that result from its use. In the first six months of 1987, PCP was mentioned in more than 3,600 emergency-room episodes across the country. In 1986, PCP caused 206 deaths. In many cases those deaths were not directly caused by the PCP itself but were the result of the freakish behavior the drug promotes. PCP users are almost as likely to be injured in auto accidents, fights, or in reckless dangerous activity, such as climbing high poles or jumping out of windows, as they are to experience a severe toxic reaction to the drug. Another cause of trouble is the use of PCP in combination with another drug, such as cocaine, marijuana, or alcohol.[8]

History

Given the many negative effects of PCP, it's no surprise that this drug is no longer legally manufactured.

PCP was first synthesized over fifty years ago. Contrary to the popular mythology that surrounds the drug, it was developed for human medical use. PCP was introduced for medical treatment in 1957. Because PCP makes users feel separate from their physical sensations, it was believed it would be an ideal anesthetic and painkiller for certain types of surgery.

PCP did prove to be effective in that way, but soon the negative effects of the drug outweighed its usefulness. Too many patients came out of surgery in an agitated, disoriented state. Some experienced hallucinations or panic. These reactions were so common that in 1965 PCP was completely withdrawn from human use.

Starting in 1967, PCP was used by veterinarians as an anesthetic for animals. That same year, it first appeared on the streets as a drug of abuse.

PCP quickly gained a reputation as a dangerous drug that produced unpredictable effects. But it began to gain greater acceptance in the drug culture as other drugs with somewhat similar effects, such as LSD, became more tightly controlled. PCP was easy to manufacture illicitly, and it could be sold cheaply. Its popularity exploded. By 1979 nearly 13 percent of all high school seniors said they had tried PCP at least once.

That same year all legal manufacture of PCP was discontinued and its use, even in veterinary medicine, ended. But by then the drug had become entrenched. Because its effects varied widely, PCP was commonly substituted for drugs being sold as heroin, cocaine, MDA, or any number of other substances.

At the same time the renegade chemists experimented with analogues of PCP. The PCP molecule is not difficult for a skilled chemist to manipulate, creating new drugs with similar effects and properties. At the National Institute on Drug Abuse, some thirty different analogues have been created for research purposes. On the street, several versions have long been available. They include PCE, PHP, PCPP, TCE, and TCP. Another related drug is ketamine. Just one-tenth as potent as PCP and shorter-acting, ketamine is still used in medical settings.

Just as PCP is used as a substitute for other drugs, ketamine or other analogues are occasionally substituted for PCP. Like other drugs sold on the street, substances marketed as PCP may be something else altogether.

Whether the drug taken is PCP, or something else that has a similar effect, many of those who have experienced those effects have decided that PCP and its analogues are drugs to be avoided. "I fear the people that are on it," says Kevin. "They have no senses."

7

Clandestine Labs

There is a character in northern California known to local drug agents as Crispy Critter. The name is an example of the black humor narcotics agents often develop, for Critter was an agonized victim of the illicit drug lab in which he worked.

He was in the midst of making methamphetamine when he became weary and sat down to doze near a can of highly flammable ether. Apparently in a neglectful state of mind, he forgot to unplug an automatic electric heater positioned nearby. When the heater clicked on, the ether burst into flames that quickly engulfed Critter.

A sidekick, trying to be helpful, doused Critter with a can full of a clear liquid—only as it happened, the liquid was not water, but acetone, which added to the fire.

Critter was horribly burned, but he did survive, and went on to serve a substantial jail term for his activities. What happened to him was, in the eyes of the authorities, almost to be expected. Out of every five labs the police discover, one is found when it explodes or bursts into flames.

"Remember," says a DEA agent, "industrial labs focus on safety and quality control. In a clandestine lab, the primary focus is on secrecy." The emphasis on secrecy and the fact that most of those who produce illegal synthetics are not trained chemists, combine to make the labs highly hazardous.

Legitimate Drug Development

The reckless work of these illicit chemists is as far outside the scientific community as we can imagine. Within the legitimate pharmaceutical industry the development and manufacture of new drugs are important activities. But in order to be marketed for human use, legally developed drugs must first win government approval. This approval is granted by the Food and Drug Administration (FDA), which requires that all new products intended for human use must pass through a rigorous three-step process.

First, the drugs are tested for safety and toxic effects exclusively in animals. Second, they are tested to see that they produce the desired effects in animals. Finally, there is a period of controlled testing in humans. This process is so exacting that it takes years for a drug to be approved.

Sometimes, in an exceptional circumstance such as the spread of the AIDS virus, steps may be taken to shorten the lengthy process necessary to approve the use of a new drug. But even then extensive testing is done by trained experts.

The fact that a drug has passed through these rigorous procedures and been approved is no guarantee that it will continue to be considered acceptable for human use. Perhaps the best-known example of a compound on which the decision was reversed is cyclamates. Once widely used to sweeten soft drinks artificially, cyclamates were withdrawn from the market in 1970 when it was determined that they might cause chromosome damage or cancer.[1]

*A house, the site of an illegal drug lab,
burns after catching fire during a drug bust.*

In the case of the illicit synthetics, there is no forum for complaint, no method of recall or control. Neither is there any long-term familiarity with the drugs and their effects, even by abusers, because underground experimentation is constantly yielding new compounds, as well as altered versions of old ones. "In essence, young drug abusers who take these new synthetics are playing a form of Russian roulette," says Robert J. Roberton, Ph.D., vice president of Drug Programs at Behavioral Health Sciences, Inc., in Los Angeles. "Only it is not lead bullets that they are aiming at their brains, but chemical ones."[2]

Cooks and Chemists

Who are the people manufacturing these synthetics? They range from motorcycle gang members to doctors and professional researchers. Those who have had extensive academic training, and who possess the knowledge and skills necessary to create new analogues by rearranging atoms, are usually known as "chemists." Among illegal drug makers, they are looked upon with considerable respect.

Another category consists of those who have learned to make certain drugs by watching their cohorts or by following simple recipes. They are called cooks. Cooks are more likely to be behind the production of drugs that are relatively easy to make, such as PCP and methamphetamine.

"Statistically," says one expert on illicit labs, "we can even give a profile of an average methamphetamine manufacturer. He is a white male and may be well educated or has spent time learning techniques from an experienced cooker. Often, this chemistry lesson takes place in prison where formulas and techniques are passed around between inmates. He may have ties to outlaw motorcycle gangs who will provide him with necessary chemicals, protection, and a ready market for the finished product.

An abandoned lab once used to make designer drugs
until it was seized by DEA agents and police

This cooker will pick an isolated area for his laboratory, where the threat from law enforcement is minimal. This week he will make approximately 24 pounds of high quality methamphetamine which he will sell for about $500,000!"[3]

Some cooks set up their labs with virtually no training. "I moved into this house with a friend of mine in Seattle," one fifteen-year-old girl explained, "and this guy was making it in the bathroom and I'm very interested. I like to learn things, so I just stayed up with him on three different nights and he would go through all the steps and I would write down how to do it. And he taught me and the next time I helped him do it. We did this around five times and I learned a lot. I can do it now, and I know most of the chemicals. I have all of it written down and I have to go by it, the temperature and everything. I couldn't remember it all. It's too complicated. And people think it's easy to do, but it's not."[4]

At the other end of the scale from this young girl and California's "statistical cooker" is the DuPont Company employee apprehended for manufacturing 3-methylfentanyl. That man held a Ph.D. in chemistry, earned a high salary from his legitimate job, and had no criminal record. (See Chapter 8 for more on this man.)

Cooking for Profits

Whether they are chemistry students, experienced doctors, or prison-educated cooks, those who make illicit drugs do so for one primary reason: the opportunity to make huge profits.

The cost of making different drugs can vary tremendously, depending on the difficulty of obtaining the necessary ingredients. Even so, the successful illicit lab can generate many thousands of dollars every week. It is estimated, for example, that it would cost about $2,000 to purchase the equipment and chemicals necessary to make 50 million doses of 3-methylfentanyl. That process would take about two weeks. The 3-methylfentanyl made would have a street value of at least $1 billion.

A small lab might make three or four pounds of methamphetamine each week, using chemicals that cost only a few hundred dollars. By the time the drug was cut and divided into dose amounts, each pound would have a street value of from $30,000 to $100,000. A larger, more sophisticated operation could produce as much as 100 pounds in a week.

Some people manufacture drugs for reasons other than money. For those who are already users, manufacturing drugs may simply be a way to feed a habit cheaply. And for those who are proud of their chemistry skills, creating new drugs or duplicating difficult-to-produce analogues is a matter of twisted pride. "It really is a scientific challenge," says Dr. Darryl Inaba, a pharmacologist with the Haight-Ashbury Free Clinics. "There's also a snobbism of these chemists who are so confident they're doing something good."

It is true that many illicit chemists believe they've earned an odd sort of prestige through their work. "I feel that I as an individual went to a great deal of trouble and expense to make sure that the materials I gave out were of good quality," said one chemist, who had been jailed for his activities. As for the risks faced by those who use the drugs, he shrugged them off. "It depends on whether or not you choose to play the game. All the people that were involved were volunteers. No one held them down and injected them."[5]

In another case, a drug agent was startled when a chemist he had arrested announced that there was one good thing about going to prison—he expected to be admired by his fellow prisoners. "He was sure of one thing," the agent recalls, "that he would be revered for his accomplishments as the 'chemist' of a large scale drug producing operation. He said that he truly felt that he was going to be a member of an elite group of the brotherhood of criminals."[6]

Clandestine labs bear little resemblance to the well-organized chemistry labs most students work in. Glass bottles, tubing, and cans of chemicals are strewn about. Large glass containers with narrow necks, known as reaction flasks, nestle into heating mantles resembling large, open crockpots. All kinds of tubes protrude from the reaction flasks and carry wastes away to glass jars or to drains. There is usually a jumble of chemical containers, electric wires strung everywhere, thermometers, and other tools.

The cooks may have a bed or cot set up in their lab work area, so they can be constantly present while the reactions are going on. Windows may be painted black or boarded up to prevent detection. The lab may be in a kitchen, a garage, a laundry room, bathroom, or converted warehouse.

Vacuum flasks filter out impurities in the drugs.

Wherever the lab is located, and whatever the details of its setup, it is a dangerous place to be. The primary hazard is the presence of toxic chemicals, often improperly labeled, improperly handled, and stored without regard for safety precautions. Many of the chemicals necessary in the production of illicit synthetics pose hazards unrelated to the problems of drug abuse.

The ether often used as a solvent is highly explosive, and acetone, another solvent, is extremely flammable. A random spark or cigarette ember will ignite either chemical in an instant. Lithium aluminum hydride, sometimes used in making crank, is also flammable—it explodes on contact with water. A drop of perspiration is enough to set it off.

One means of making methamphetamine requires the use of a device called a hydrogenator, normally used in the manufacture of perfume. It also requires a tank of hydrogen, such as might be used in welding. The resulting setup is nothing less than a bomb, waiting to be ignited by the forgetful person who strikes a match or makes an electrical spark by flicking a light switch.

The procedure for making PCP involves the use of two chemicals that if accidentally mixed form deadly cyanide gas. Also, hydrofluoric acid, normally used in etching glass, has been found in labs. If spilled on the skin it doesn't hurt because it anesthetizes the nerves as it eats through flesh to the bone.

Even highly trained legitimate chemists can't predict what toxic fumes might result when certain drugs are combined. These unknown fumes are sometimes referred to as mutant chemical atmospheres. They represent just one more unknown danger that may be found in clandestine labs.

Poisonous chemicals such as cyanide powder, mercury, or cancer-causing methylamine are routinely found in labs. "We're talking about something that people could walk through and die," says one drug agent. "I've never worked anything with the dangers of clandestine labs. As far as I'm concerned, this is the most dangerous thing in law enforcement a guy can do."

It is equally dangerous for those who work in or enter labs. The notorious Crispy Critter survived his lab's explosion, but not all the drug makers are so lucky. It is not unusual for cooks to die in their labs, victims of toxic fumes or even substances they have absorbed through the skin. "They die from being spaced out and doing the wrong things," says a drug agent.

In addition to the effects of chemicals accidentally inhaled or unknowingly absorbed through the skin, the cooks and chemists suffer from the effects of their illicit product. The West Coast chemist who manufactured the MPTP-contaminated MPPP that caused Parkinson's disease in many of its users also fell victim to that illness.

For the police who seek out labs, the chemical dangers are only the beginning. Clandestine labs are often guarded by firearm-wielding cooks—and firearms are even more dangerous in a lab because the flash they produce when fired can ignite any one of many explosive chemicals likely to be present.

Cooks often set booby traps to protect them from unwanted intruders or from police. The booby trap may be a light fixture filled with a chemical that will burst into flames when the switch is flipped, a refrigerator wired to explode when the door is opened, or something as simple as a can of powerful acid balanced on a partially open doorway.

Environmental Hazards
of Labs

The toxic effects of a lab's presence are not limited to those who actually enter the lab while it is operating. Escaping fumes pollute the area dangerously, exposing

Agents with the Drug Enforcement Administration
dismantle a methamphetamine lab in northern
California. The agents wear special breathing
apparatus as well as protective shoes and over-
garments. Clandestine labs are often filled with
toxic fumes, such as cyanide gas. Many of the
chemicals found in these labs, such as mercury
or lead acetate, may be absorbed through the
skin if accidentally touched.

people nearby to the toxic effects of the drug being manufactured and its by-products.

As the illicit drugs are produced, many of the substances needed to complete the process are left over. Some of the chemicals, such as mercury or cyanide powder, may remain on the floors and counters long after the drug making is finished. These chemicals are not removed during normal cleaning. Methamphetamine waste, mercury salts, cyanide wastes, and lead salts are all dangerous substances. They can remain viable and present, even in soil, for years. New occupants of buildings that have housed labs risk exposure to these poisons. Even people picnicking in areas where toxic materials have been dumped are in danger.

Many cooks dispose of their dangerous wastes by simply pouring them down the toilet. But these powerful chemicals can disable a sewage processing plant. In one case, DEA agents were alerted to the presence of a drug lab when all the grass in a park area died after being irrigated with water from a nearby treatment plant. The plant had become contaminated with chemicals that the agents recognized as being among those often found in drug labs.[7]

In rural areas the chemical wastes can kill the bacteria necessary in septic systems. As a result, hazardous chemicals and raw sewage may leach out, contaminating aquifers and water sources. Such wastes dumped into lakes or streams can cause hazardous levels of pollution. Buried in containers they pose a threat to those who may accidentally come into contact with them when the containers decompose or are later uncovered.

These concerns are very real. In 1987 the California Health Commission declared the location of an illicit lab that had been closed two years earlier to be a toxic site. But drug agents estimate that they locate only about one out of every ten labs in operation. Which chemicals the undiscovered labs are pouring into the environment may never be known. But the effects of those chemicals are likely to become apparent, as we see the resulting pollution, illness, and perhaps even deaths.

8
Trafficking the Synthetics

In 1985 a DuPont Company chemist was arrested for manufacturing and distributing $1 million worth of fentanyl. In fact, the chemist's main sale was to the Drug Enforcement Administration (DEA). The man had been set up for a "sting" almost as soon as he had synthesized his illicit product.[1]

"He was a very sophisticated chemist," says Ray McKinnon, chief of the DEA's Dangerous Drug Investigation section. "He had the ability to make 3-methylfentanyl, but he had no idea how to be a criminal."[2]

As McKinnon recalls, the chemist tried to find customers by sending notes describing the drug to a long-haired co-worker. The co-worker, fearful that perhaps *he* was being set up for an arrest, immediately informed his superiors. The DEA was brought in, and the chemist was done for.

The story sounds as if the chemist was almost unbelievably inept, but in fact his problem was not unusual. It is not easy to dispose of millions of doses of an illicit drug. "People think that if they can make drugs, that's just great, they'll make a million dollars," says Dr. Gary Henderson. "But it takes more than the ability to make it. Distribution is the key. It's like the most fundamental concept in economics—marketing. You can have the best product and if you can't market it, it goes nowhere."

All illicit drugs are distributed in the same basic way. The only difference is that illicit synthetics are manufactured in domestic labs.

Most drugs are bought on the street in small quantities. But before a drug reaches the individual user, it has passed through many hands and been diluted many times. The dealer on the street or the school campus is at the low end of a pyramid structured much like other businesses.

From Top to Bottom

At the top of the pyramid is the financier—the individual who supplies the start-up money. Occasionally a cook will operate completely independently, but more often he or she will need some financial assistance to get set up.

The financier may be a person who doesn't use drugs and doesn't want to handle the drugs or have any direct association with them. He or she may work exclusively with one cook or may back several. In addition to providing money, the financier may also provide the cook with the names of contacts who can oversee the distribution of several pounds of the illicit drug each week.

Normally the cook will produce methamphetamine that is 80 to 100 percent pure. The drug is then passed along to a select group of lieutenants. They may also be called "pound men" because one pound is the smallest amount they are willing to sell. The cook is likely to know of three or four such people, each of whom will buy five to ten pounds a week.

Because they are dealing regularly, the cooker may give these high-level customers their portion of the drug on consignment. This is an honor system under which the lieutenants take the drug without paying anything, and when they have made their sales they pay the cook. The cook, in turn, passes along whatever percentage is due back to the financier.

The lieutenants' first action is to dilute the drug down to a purity of about 60 percent. Five pounds of powder instantly become eight pounds, and the profits are also proportionately increased.

Once this is done, the lieutenants offer their product to a small group of regular customers. Just as the cook deals only with well-known lieutenants, the lieutenants are most likely to sell their pounds to a limited circle of familiar customers.

The drug dealers who buy pounds also dilute, or "step on," their product. They divide it into ounces or half-ounces and offer their ware to a larger number of customers. It may be cut yet again by these lower-level dealers, but they then try to ensure that the drug that reaches the user has enough purity to provide a good high.

An ounce is still quite a lot of drug. There are twenty-eight grams in one ounce. In the case of methamphetamine, a very heavy user might consume one gram in the course of a day, but for the lighter user a normal dose amount would be one-eighth of a gram or even less.

Thus, the drug may pass through many hands before it reaches the final user, each time being cut with unknown substances and measured less precisely. At the bottom of the dealer line is the user who may buy half a gram, consuming part and selling the rest for just enough profit to support his or her own habit. Or, the dealer may be an underage person working for a slightly older boss.

At the bottom of the drug trafficking pyramid it's not unusual to find dealers as young as eight or nine.[3] "You get a lot of kids, fourteen, fifteen or sixteen, doing heavy dope deals," says Dr. Charles Ladley, professor of criminal justice at California State University–Sacramento. "If they get busted they go to Juvenile Hall for a week and that's it."[4]

But Dr. Ladley also points out that the bottom of the pyramid doesn't necessarily mean young dealers. "You'll find people who are closer to the ages of the users selling to these different groups," he says. "Thirty-year-olds sell to thirty-year-olds, those in their twenties sell to others in their twenties, teens sell to teens."

Teen Sales

Among teenagers, Dr. Ladley has found, almost anyone could be selling drugs. "It could be the star athlete," he says. "He could be a distributor, though he may say he's only doing it for a few of his friends."

In high schools, some students may look upon possession of drugs as a status symbol. The drugs may be given away to a circle of friends, rather than being sold, or they may be traded for goods or services.

One California drug counselor has watched the teen drug trade near her home. "It's incredible," she says of the trafficking going on at a small nearby market. "They'll call their connection from a phone booth and a few moments later a car arrives and the exchange takes place."[5]

The dealer, teenaged or older, who is working from the bottom of the pyramid is likely to know of several connections—people willing to sell in amounts of a gram or less. They may operate out of a seemingly legitimate business, such as a mobile lunch van or a motorcycle shop; they may carry beepers and respond to phone calls from their customers; or they may hang out at specific spots in shopping malls or on the school grounds.

Sometimes the connection can supply the drugs immediately, but may equally often have to scramble for a day or two to fill the order.

Most connections have sources that provide them with many different drugs, although they have no control over the availability. The experienced user may want one particular drug and be unwilling to accept a substitute knowingly. But the young person who just wants to get high or loaded is usually happy to accept any one of several drugs. More and more frequently, such a buyer prefers to use different drugs in combination in a desperate effort to achieve the best possible high.

Because the gram dealer has so many contacts, the greatest risk of being busted exists at this level of the traffic pyramid. In order to unload the product, the gram dealer must literally sell to dozens of people. His or her identity is likely to be known to dozens more. One drug agent described with amazement a dealer whose home he once staked out. "He had visits from 250 *different* automobiles in one month," says the agent. "That's not even counting cars that came back again and again. To warrant that many visits he had to be selling in grams, half grams, maybe even quarter grams. Those are tiny amounts."[6]

Dealer Security

Those at the upper levels of the pyramid would never consider such broad contacts. They remain carefully compartmentalized, their identities known only to the very limited circle in which they deal directly. The low-level dealer has no idea who cooked the drug, who the lieutenants or pound men are. The dealer is always willing to vouch for the quality of the product, but is so far removed from its source that there is no way to know what it actually is, how often it has been cut, or what substances have been used in the process. The pound men and lieutenants, in turn, haven't the slightest interest in the street or school-yard dealers.

"Some groups are very good about compartmentalization," says Ray McKinnon. "On the West Coast, the Hell's Angels control much of the methamphetamine traffic. They have separate groups handling the precursors, cooking, trafficking, and distribution. You may get one, but he can't tell you any information about the overall operation."

In some cities, such as Philadelphia, organized crime has taken control of the distribution of methamphetamine and other synthetics. Although the big crime syndicates have long dominated the market for heroin and cocaine, they are just beginning to move in on the field of illicit synthetics. In other areas street gangs sometimes handle much of the small-scale distribution of certain drugs within their turf areas. But the synthetics may also be manufactured and distributed by independents who have no outside bonds or obligations.

Precursor Traffic

Precursors are chemicals used in making designer drugs. The business of moving precursor chemicals from one location to another has also created an opportunity for profit. In most cases the needed chemicals are simply purchased in a state in which they are perfectly legal and transported to another state. As more states restrict the availability of the chemicals needed to make synthetic drugs, the chemists are likely to counter by developing new processes using different, legal substances.

Interstate and International Trafficking

Finally, synthetics traffic is extremely difficult to control because drugs can be spread from one area to another by simply providing a new cooker with a recipe. "The recipe is a very marketable item," says McKinnon.

Recipes may be shared among prison inmates, friends, or casual acquaintances. Some are guarded jealously; others are occasionally sold for profit. Since anyone who obtains a recipe can manufacture the drug, it hardly seems

necessary to move large amounts of any synthetic drug between distant places. And yet it does happen.

Although methamphetamine labs have been found in some two dozen states, California is the center of this activity. Police theorize that about two tons (eighteen hundred kilograms) of the drug are made in California each week. It would be almost impossible for it all to be consumed there.

In many cases the lieutenants transport it to other areas by the simplest of means—they pack it in trunks and ship it by train, they load it into the trunks of their cars and drive it away, or they even mail it. Unless they have already been placed under police surveillance, the chances of detection are slim.

Texas is another major manufacturing center, particularly for MDMA. MDMA use is becoming increasingly widespread in the midwestern states, and police report it is becoming more readily available on the West Coast. Much of this drug is being shipped out from Texas labs.

The quantities being produced are so tremendous, particularly in the case of methamphetamine, that the United States is now in the odd position of exporting illicit drugs.

ABOVE: *state troopers stand outside a Hell's Angels clubhouse following a raid on the premises by state and federal law enforcement authorities.* BELOW: *a member of the Hell's Angels Motorcycle Club (with arms behind his back) is arrested by FBI agents. That day more than 125 people in over 50 locations were arrested for violations of the Controlled Substance Act and the Racketeer Influenced and Corrupt Organizations Act.*

DEA officials believe that methamphetamine made in California is being shipped to Korea, Thailand, and Japan.

The ease with which the synthetics are manufactured and distributed is a problem that frustrates law enforcement agencies at every level. How do you block the availability of drugs that can be made by an amateur chemist using perfectly legal materials? "I don't think we're looking at stopping it," says Ray McKinnon. "We're trying to control it—to keep it within a manageable level."

9
The New Synthetics and the Law

In 1982, when a group of drug users in San Jose, California, developed the terrible symptoms of Parkinson's disease, it was a major medical mystery. But one aspect of the story was never mysterious at all. Once police were informed the illness was being caused by MPPP contaminated with MPTP, they quickly learned the source of the drug.

Authorities knew the identity of the chemist. They had even inspected his lab. However, there was little they could do about his activities. Under the laws in effect in 1982, the man was doing nothing illegal.

To understand the special challenge that the emergence of synthetic drug analogues has posed for law enforcement agencies, it is helpful to examine the way our anti-drug laws have been structured.

The Controlled Substances Act

One of the most significant laws was passed in 1970. The Controlled Substances Act defined categories of drugs that might be abused and laid out strict guidelines regarding the use and availability of drugs within those categories, or schedules.

Decisions to control a particular substance at the federal level are normally made by the Drug Enforcement Administration or the Department of Health and Human Services. Officials from those agencies must gather information on many aspects of the drug involved. Among the factors they examine are the drug's potential for abuse, the body of scientific knowledge about the substance, its current level of use on the street, and any risk it poses to public health. The more dangerous the drug, the more restricted its availability and the more severe the penalties for trafficking.[1]

If it is decided that a particular drug should be regulated, it is placed on one of five schedules. The most tightly controlled drugs are those in Schedule I. They are believed to have a high potential for abuse and have no currently accepted medical use. They are also considered potentially unsafe, even when given by a doctor. The federal penalty for trafficking some of these drugs ranges up to twenty years, even for a first offense. Schedule I drugs include heroin, LSD, MDMA, and even marijuana.

Schedule II drugs are also considered prime drugs of abuse, whose use is likely to lead to severe psychological or physical dependence. These drugs may, however, have some medically accepted use, although such use is likely to be tightly controlled. Among the drugs in Schedule II are cocaine, PCP, amphetamines, and some barbiturates.

Schedule III drugs include both sedatives and stimulants with a commonly accepted medical use. Although these drugs are sometimes abused, they are believed less likely to result in physical addiction.

More commonly prescribed drugs, such as Valium, Librium, some mild stimulants, and sleep aids, are classified in Schedules IV and V. Their medical use is well accepted, and their potential for abuse is considered lower than that of drugs in the other categories.

The Effects of Scheduling

Unfortunately, scheduling drugs does not do much to stop users who will risk anything to get high at any price. "The problem," says one DEA agent, "is that you only legislate the decent people. They're the only ones who are going to pay attention."

Matters weren't helped by the fact that until new legislation was passed in 1986, the scheduling process was lengthy and complicated. It easily took a year or more to schedule a particular drug. In that time, an experimental new drug could come and go.

That is, in fact, what happened. Under the Controlled Substances Act, the scheduled drugs were defined in the most precise way—according to their actual molecular structure. Yet as we have seen in the case of the fentanyl analogues, it's possible to create a new drug, just one or two atoms different from the parent drug. The effects of that new analogue may be far more potent than those of the parent drug. Even so, as a new drug not listed in the government schedules, the substance can be used legally.

Thus, when authorities visited the San Jose chemist they believed to be making contaminated MPPP, the main grounds for their search were that the chemicals stored on his property were a fire hazard. The chemist showed them his lab, explaining that he was experimenting with moisturizers and new flavors for snowcones. That story didn't coincide with the chemicals present—gallons of ether and acetone among them. A pinch of white powder taken away from the site was analyzed and found to be a narcotic substance.[2] But there were no grounds for prosecution.

Because of this legal loophole, the mid-eighties were a

time of much illicit experimentation. The chemists were able to track the scheduling procedures of the drugs they were producing. The minute a particular analogue was scheduled, they could move on to produce yet another variation. For a time, the new analogue would be completely legal.

A typical example of such a process was apparent in the case of MDMA. In 1985, the DEA was given "emergency scheduling authority." This meant that a drug with strong potential for abuse could be scheduled before the detailed scientific analysis had been completed. The procedure still took months, but it was far quicker than anything that could be accomplished under the old rules.

New Legislation

This gap in the law was finally closed with the passage of the Anti–Drug Abuse Act of 1986. That legislation included a section, the Controlled Substance Analogue Enforcement Act of 1986, devoted specifically to the problem of illicit analogues. Under the new law, analogues of controlled drugs are to be treated in precisely the same way as those drugs listed in Schedule I under the Controlled Substances Act. Possessing, selling, or manufacturing them is therefore illegal, even if their chemical structure has not been previously classified.

According to the new law, any analogue with a chemical structure similar to that of a prohibited drug may be considered illegal. In addition, any drug that has been created to produce the effects of a stimulant, depressant, or hallucinogen may be illegal. Individuals may also be prosecuted for selling drugs that they *claim* have those effects, even though the claims may be false.

The Controlled Substance Analogue Enforcement Act has been carefully written to allow for normal scientific investigation and the legitimate development of new drugs. At this writing, the law has not been fully tested in the courts, and it is hard to predict exactly what its impact on the manufacture and distribution of illicit synthetics will be.

The Growing Number
of Labs

One possible effect could be that the chemists will simply turn their energies away from the development of new analogues and instead focus on those products they know can be easily sold. In 1987, DEA officials closed nearly seven hundred labs. Most of those were producing methamphetamine. In 1988 DEA officials expected to close an even greater number of labs.

The vast numbers mean that illicit labs have become the number-two DEA priority in many of the agency's regions—only the cocaine problem is considered more serious. Even so, those figures represent only the lab seizures in which DEA agents played a role. Labs seized by state or local officials are not represented on any national tally.

Going After Labs

Seizing, or "taking down," labs is one of the key ways enforcement officials at every level are combatting the spread of synthetics. But for every lab they identify and seize, agents estimate that as many as ten continue operating.

Nationally, labs of various types have been discovered in some three dozen states. Tracking them down and dismantling them properly constitute a whole new area of law enforcement. It requires special training, not only for the police who may enter a lab, but for firemen who may be called when a chemical fire rages and for the experts who will need to dispose of toxic wastes while preserving vital evidence.

There are some regions of the country where few labs have been seized, but, says DEA's Ray McKinnon, that's no reason to suppose that labs aren't operating. "Some areas have not yet addressed the problem. If you don't look for labs, you don't find them."

Tracking Labs

Those who do look for labs have learned there are many ways of finding them. As we have seen, some are discovered when they burst into flames. But even an apparently destroyed lab is likely to yield enough evidence to convict its operators.

The presence of a clandestine lab may also be revealed by the simplest of neighborly complaints. Some labs produce incredibly foul odors. The neighbor's official protest can be an important clue to police. The odd behavior of the illicit chemists can also draw the attention of the authorities. One large-scale California lab was raided when police were tipped off by neighbors who noticed that the "handyman" wore an automatic rifle strapped across his back whenever he mowed the lawn!

Narcotics agents infiltrate the operation of clandestine labs, just as they do narcotics smuggling cartels. Many agents are well versed in the details of drug manufacture and have sometimes succeeded in hiring themselves out as "cooks" for eager financiers.

Another way of uncovering labs is by tracing the purchase of needed ingredients. Sometimes a slightly odd purchase may attract attention. Mercuric chloride is required for some processes. Another key element is common aluminum foil. Cooks have been caught after purchasing rolls of aluminum foil by the case.

Police seize a California lab

In other cases, they make their activities known when they buy precursor chemicals. Many of these chemicals do have legitimate industrial use. Phenylacetic acid, for example, is used in some processes for making methamphetamine. It is also important in the manufacture of penicillin molds and may be used in perfumes. Methylamine, also used in making methamphetamine, can be an ingredient in insecticides or fuels. Ether and acetone have many industrial uses.

When such chemicals are purchased by legal businesses, orders are normally placed in advance and paid for by check or purchase order. Chemical supply houses are well aware that the customer who comes in off the street and buys large amounts of certain chemicals with cash probably intends to use them for illicit purposes.

Some chemical supply houses tip off police, but others have learned that dealing with the clandestine lab operators can be a good way to make a profit. Such store operators have found that the illicit chemists are willing to pay a premium for the chemicals they need.

Precursor Control

One way to put a damper on such chemical sales is to control the distribution of known precursors, even as some drugs are controlled. For example, P2P (phenyl-2-propanone), an important methamphetamine precursor, is now a federally controlled substance. PCC (1-piperidino-cyclohexane carbonitrile), a precursor to PCP, is also federally controlled. In states where lab activity is high, such as California, a variety of chemicals are regulated. The process of controlling a chemical does not make it unavailable for legitimate use. It simply means that careful records of sales must be kept, and buyers must be prepared to explain what use they will make of their chemical purchases.

When ingredients are hard to come by, chemists have a special response. They simply develop new processes for creating their drugs. As P2P and methylamine became hard to obtain, California cooks started making methamphetamine using ephedrine, a substance that could be legally purchased by anyone. It is a common ingredient in nasal inhalers.

Eventually ephedrine was controlled in California, but the regulation of all items that could be used in the manufacture of illicit drugs is simply not possible. According to Dr. Gary Henderson, "A determined chemist can still find materials, because eventually you would have to outlaw any organic chemical. The new laws make it more difficult, but they do not make it impossible to make drugs."

10
The Impact
of Synthetics

As this book was being written, new synthetics were appearing on the streets. U4EUH (an abbreviation for euphoria) and 2-CB (similar to U4EUH) are among those of which authorities have recently become aware. But little is known about these drugs, other than the fact that they are becoming more available to street users.

No one can say how many other such experimental synthetics may be in circulation. Unless a drug has attracted at least a small following of abusers, it is unlikely to become known to the scientific community.

The Role of Synthetics

The most effective way to deal with the hazards of the synthetics is to eliminate their use. But that means solving the problem of drug abuse completely, and no such solution is yet in sight. In fact, after a period of declining drug use, some indicators show that the drug problem is once again on the rise. As the illicit synthetics become more available, will they play a role in increasing drug use?

The answer to that question depends on many factors. Drug users are not automatically attracted to new "products." Many, in fact, refuse to use anything that seems unfamiliar. "I've known users to turn down crank because it was the wrong color," says one drug agent. "Even though it was exactly the same as what they'd been using, they wouldn't take it."

Such customer response provides dealers with a strong motive for disguising their synthetic products as other, well-known substances. It also means that a newly developed drug will not necessarily develop a large following, no matter what effects it produces. The experienced street drug user almost always prefers to stay with something familiar.

But the selling of drugs is a business, and the economic factor may play a role in the expanding use of synthetics. "If the government were able to block the importation of cocaine into this country," says Dr. Gary Henderson, "we'd have synthetic cocaine on the street in a month. If the government were to block the importation of heroin, it would be completely taken over by the synthetics. If the natural product is cheap and available they'll use that. As long as black tar heroin is literally as cheap as dirt, and as long as cocaine is cheaper than marijuana, there will not be a big drive for the synthetics."

It is ironic that the more successful law enforcement efforts to block the importation of illicit drugs become, the more likely it is that the abuse of synthetics will expand. In some views, that expansion is virtually inevitable. "The domestic production of new, potent synthetic drugs will be the major drug abuse problem in the future," says Dr. Robert Roberton. "As efforts to control natural products such as opium, coca and marijuana become more successful, and as safeguards to prevent the diversion of pharmaceuticals become more effective, there will be more incentive for the illicit synthesis of drugs like fentanyl. New synthetic drugs will appear which will be more

*More than nine tons of confiscated
heroin, opium, marijuana, and other
drugs about to be set afire by police.
Although efforts have increased to
control availability of these drugs,
the manufacture of designer drugs
may be more difficult to control.*

potent and more selective in their action. Smoking and snorting these drugs will become more popular."

In that development, Roberton believes, the potential for significant trouble lurks. "Drug users become guinea pigs when each new batch hits the streets," he says.[1]

Cycles of Abuse

Some experts believe that certain patterns of drug abuse in society are repeated again and again. "Historically there is an upper-downer syndrome," says Dr. Darryl Inaba. "All drugs are abused at any given time. But the focus tends to swing from uppers to downers. It happens because the body can't tolerate long periods of high doses of stimulants."

In the 1970s, Dr. Inaba says, the street outside his Haight-Ashbury office was "a desolation row for downers —depressant and sedative drugs."

That scene has changed dramatically. "We are currently in an upper cycle," he says. "In this cycle cocaine has been emphasized. But in the cycle people will turn to a more practical drug, and that's crank."

If the patterns of abuse continue as Dr. Inaba anticipates, the shift in the 1990s will be back toward depressants. Right now, he says, more and more drugs are turning up in a smokable form. An example is methamphetamine. Normally it is taken orally, snorted, or injected, but in 1986 a new, smokable version of the drug appeared on the street.

The change, produced by illicit chemists, was the response to a desire for something Dr. Inaba calls "pharmaceutical eloquence." This refers to the actual experience of taking the drug, as opposed to the effects it causes. Methamphetamine is normally an unpleasant-tasting substance that can be uncomfortable to snort and painful to inject. "Smoking crank is a more pleasant way of abusing the drug," Dr. Inaba explains.

But if the cycle continues as he anticipates, the popularity of methamphetamine will wane in the next few years, only to be replaced by something else. According to his theory, that substance is likely to be a smokable form of heroin.

Levels of Use

Although certain drugs may come and go, it is clear that in recent years the overall number of users has increased tremendously. According to a report issued by the American Psychiatric Association, in the early 1960s only 2 percent of the population had experimented with illicit psychoactive drugs. By 1982 some 30 percent of household population age twelve and over had some experience with those drugs. An estimated 60 million Americans had tried marijuana, and some 20 million continued to be regular users. It was also estimated that 20 million Americans had tried cocaine, and 4 million continued to be regular users. The number has increased substantially since then.[2]

There is no way to know precisely how many people are using or have chosen to experiment with illicit drugs. Some statistics are generated through reports from hospital emergency rooms, but as drug users grow more knowledgeable about the drugs they take, they are less likely to report to such facilities.

Other surveys depend on questionnaires, which count on the drug user to be open and honest in responding. Unfortunately, those who do abuse drugs are often unwilling to participate in surveys. Thus, the information we get from even the most carefully collected statistics is bound to be incomplete at best.

Why Choose to Use?

There is, however, a growing understanding of why many young people decide to experiment with drugs. A recent study of high school sophomores conducted by Stanford University found that the key factor in a teenager's decision about using drugs is the attitude of other teenagers.[3] "It's not how many teenagers are using drugs," says Tom Robinson, a researcher on the project, "but how many a teenager *thinks* are using drugs. And kids' perceptions are greater than actual use."

The Stanford study found that the same pressures make it hard to decide against substance abuse, whether the item involved is a cigarette, an alcoholic drink, or a drug. "We teach kids first to identify the social factors that influence them," says Robinson. "Perhaps it's a boyfriend who smokes marijuana. The idea then is to plot a strategy to deal with that pressure." First, says Robinson, a young person must determine which situations present a temptation to use drugs—whether it's being with a particular special friend, a party situation, or the fact that drugs are frequently used in certain situations.

Once the situation is identified, the teenager plans exactly how he or she will respond the next time it occurs. This includes deciding what to say and practicing the best response to anyone who offers drugs.

Persuading people not to use drugs, according to Robinson, is just the first step. "The important thing is to help them develop the skills to be able to resist."

Deciding Against
Drug Use

Developing such skills is even more important, given the emergence of the illicit synthetics. It is now apparent that as long as people want to take illicit drugs, those drugs will be available. In this day of kitchen laboratories, it's a simple matter of supply and demand. Says Dr. Ronald Siegel, "Unless you outlaw the science of cooking and chemistry and gardening, you will never eliminate mind-altering drugs."[4]

Recognizing the hazards of all illicit drugs, and the increased dangers of the synthetics in particular, is one important step. But the second step, the step away from drugs, is the one that will matter most in the long run.

Hotlines

What should you do if you have a problem with drugs, or if you know someone who does? A good first step is to call one of the many hotlines set up to provide information and assistance to those who need it.

The people who staff these hotlines will not ask for names, or for any other personal information you don't care to give. They're there to provide you with accurate information. In many cases they'll be able to direct you to medical services in your area, including some that are free.

For additional, local telephone numbers, look in your Yellow Pages under "Drug Abuse" or "Drug Treatment."

Hotlines

1-800-662-HELP: NIDA Hotline. Refers callers to sources of assistance in their local areas; provides free materials on drug abuse.

1-800-COCAINE: Around-the-clock counseling and information from reformed cocaine users. Sometimes criticized as a marketing tool for the affiliated hospital, 800-COCAINE is still a valuable resource for the person who needs help.

1-800-556-CARE: CareUnit National Treatment System. Refers callers to treatment facilities within their local area.

Information: Call the Information operator for the number of the State Substance Abuse Office in your state.

Check your telephone directory for listings of:

Narcotics Anonymous

Starting Point

Alateen

Al-Anon

For other local clinics, treatment programs, and general information, check your telephone book Yellow Pages.

Information

1-800-554-KIDS: The National Federation of Parents for Drug Free Youth (NFP). Information and referrals for parents concerned about preventing drug problems in young people, as well as those whose children are already involved with drugs.

1-800-241-9746: PRIDE Drug Information Line. Parent's Resource Institute for Drug Education (PRIDE) provides drug information, helps parents form groups in their own community, and offers drug information tapes after business hours.

Notes

Chapter Two

1. Rudy M. Baum, "Designer Drugs," *Chemical and Engineering News,* 9 Sept. 1985, 15.
2. "The Frozen Addict," *Nova,* telecast, Public Broadcasting System, 1986.
3. Matt Clark and Nancy Stadtman, "A Bad Drug's Benefit," *Newsweek,* 9 Dec. 1985.
4. Dr. J. William Langston, interview with author, 9 Sept. 1987.
5. Senate Subcommittee on Children, Family, Drugs and Alcoholism of the Committee on Labor and Human Resources, *Designer Drugs, 1985,* 25 July 1985, 31.
6. J. M. Wright, R. A. Wall, T. L. Perry, and D. W. Paty, "Chronic Parkinsonism Secondary to Intranasal Administration of a Product of Meperidine Analog Synthesis," *New England Journal of Medicine,* vol. 310, 2 Feb. 1984, 325.
7. Dr. Darryl Inaba, interview with author, 10 July 1987.
8. Dr. Gary Henderson, interview with author, 13 July 1987.

Chapter Three

1. Senate Subcommittee on Children, Family, Drugs and Alcoholism, *Investigating the Threat of Designer Drugs and Efforts to Stop Them,* 25 July 1985, 56.

2. Jack Schafer, "Designer Drugs," *Science 85* (Mar. 1985), 66.
3. Melanie Kirsch, *Designer Drugs* (Minneapolis, Minn: CompCare, 1986), 38–39.
4. Drug counselor, interview with author, 27 Jan. 1988.
5. DEA agent, interview with author, 18 Aug. 1987.
6. Subcommittee on Children, Family, Drugs and Alcoholism, *Designer Drugs, 1985*, 11.
7. Peter Kerr, "Study: Drugs Play Key Crime Role," *Sacramento Bee*, 22 Jan. 1988, A19.
8. Winifred Gallagher, "The Looming Menace of Designer Drugs," *Discover* (Aug. 1986), 32–33.
9. Dr. Gary Henderson, interview with author, 13 July 1987.
10. William A. Ayres, Mary Jo Starsiak, Phil Sokolay, "The Bogus Drug: Three Methyl & Alpha Methyl Fentanyl Sold as 'China White,'" *Journal of Psychoactive Drugs* 19 (Jan.–Mar. 1981), 91.

Chapter Four

1. G. Ricaurte, G. Bryan, L. Strauss, L. Seiden, and C. Schuster, "Hallucinogenic Amphetamine Selectively Destroys Brain Serotonin Nerve Terminals," *Science*, 6 Sept. 1985, 986.
2. Dr. Thomas Streed, interview with author, 23 July 1987.
3. Ibid.
4. National Institute on Drug Abuse, *Community Epidemiology Work Group Executive Summary*, June 1986.
5. National Institute on Drug Abuse, *Highlights, 1985 National Household Survey on Drug Abuse*.
6. Edward M. Brecher and the editors of *Consumer Reports* magazine, *Licit and Illicit Drugs* (Boston: Little, Brown, 1952), 278.
7. Ibid.
8. Ibid., 282.

Chapter Five

1. Kathryn Gertz, " 'Hug Drug' Alert: The Agony of Ecstasy," *Harper's Bazaar* (Nov. 1985), 50.
2. Dr. Ronald Siegel, interview with author, 28 July 1987.
3. Lewis Seiden and Charles Schuster, "The Neurotoxicity of Amphetamines and Their Derivatives" (paper), University of Chicago, 16 Jan. 1986.
4. G. T. Dowling, E. T. McDonough, R. O. Bost, "Eve and Ecstasy: Report of Five Deaths," *Journal of the American Medical Association* 257 (27 Mar. 1987), 1615–17.

5. Senate Subcommittee on Children, Family, Drugs and Alcoholism of the Committee on Labor and Human Resources, *Designer Drugs, 1985*, 25 July 1985, 79.

6. Christina Parker, "The Politics of 'Ecstasy,' " *Designer Drugs* (Phoenix, Ariz.: Do It Now Foundation, Nov./Dec., 1985).

7. Lester Grinspoon and J. B. Bakalar, "Can Drugs Be Used to Enhance the Psychotherapeutic Process?" *American Journal of Psychotherapy* 40 (July 1986), 393.

8. Gregory Haynor and Howard McKinney, "MDMA: The Dark Side of Ecstasy," *Journal of Psychoactive Drugs* 18 (Oct.–Dec. 1986).

9. Gertz, " 'Hug Drug' Alert," 50.

Chapter Six

1. S. O. Isaacs, P. Martin, J. A. Washington, *Oral Surgery, Oral Medicine, Oral Pathology* 61 (7 July 1984), 126.

2. William Chaze, "The Deadly Path of Today's PCP Epidemic," *U.S. News & World Report,* 7 July 1984, 65.

3. Orm Aniline and Ferris N. Pitts, Jr., "PCP: A Review and Perspectives," *CRC Critical Reviews in Toxicology* (April 1982), 146.

4. David H. Fram and Nancy Stone, "Clinical Observations in the Treatment of Adolescent and Young Adult PCP Abusers," *Phencyclidine: An Update* (Washington: National Institute on Drug Abuse, 1986), 255.

5. James E. Lewis and Robert B. Hordan, "Neuropsychological Assessment of Phencyclidine Abusers," *Phencyclidine: An Update* (Washington: National Institute on Drug Abuse, 1986), 193.

6. G. More, "Angel Dust Clobbers Immune Cells," *Science News,* 7 July 1984, 6.

7. Dr. Lloyd Johnston, University of Michigan, Institute for Social Research, study on illicit drug use by American high school seniors, released 20 Feb. 1987. News release by the University of Michigan News and Information Services.

8. National Narcotics Intelligence Consumers Committee, "The Supply of Illicit Drugs to the United States from Foreign and Domestic Sources in 1985 and 1986," *The NNICC Report, 1985–86.*

Chapter Seven

1. "The Sweet Stuff: An Update on Artificial Sweeteners," *Current Health* (Jan. 1985), 16.

2. Senate Subcommittee on Children, Family, Drugs and Alcoholism of the Committee on Labor and Human Resources, *Designer Drugs, 1985*, 25 July 1985, 29.

3. California Senate Select Committee on Drug and Alcohol Abuse, *Interim Hearings on Clandestine Laboratories/Designer Drugs,* testimony of Karen Dallosta, 5 Nov. 1985.
4. Edward M. Brecher, *Licit and Illicit Drugs* (Boston: Little, Brown, 1972), 300.
5. Clandestine chemist, "Designer Drugs," *The Phil Donahue Show,* Sep. 1986, transcript no. 09116, p. 6.
6. California State Senate Select Committee, *Interim Hearings,* 5 Nov. 1985.
7. Travis Brown and Glenn Brank, "Illicit Labs Leave Deadly Legacy —Toxic Chemical Wastes," *Sacramento Bee,* 8 Apr. 1986.

Chapter Eight

1. Mary Thornton and Michael Hovey, "Chemist held in designer drug scheme," *Washington Post,* 19 Dec. 1985.
2. Ray McKinnon, chief, Dangerous Drug Investigation Section, DEA, interview with author, 17 July 1987.
3. Senate Subcommittee on Children, Family, Drugs and Alcoholism, *Designer Drugs, 1985,* 25 July 1985, 58.
4. Dr. Charles Ladley, interview with author, 12 Aug. 1987.
5. Drug counselor, interview with author, 13 Aug. 1987.
6. Agent, California Bureau of Narcotics Enforcement, interview with author, 13 Aug. 1987.

Chapter Nine

1. Drug Enforcement Administration, *Drugs of Abuse,* 1987, 6–7.
2. Jack Shafer, "Designer Drugs," *Science,* Mar. 1985, 65.

Chapter Ten

1. Robert J. Roberton, text or a speech, "Designer Drugs: The Analog Game," *Narcotics Control Digest,* 3 Apr. 1985, 15.
2. American Psychiatric Association, "Position Statement on Psychoactive Substance Use and Dependence: Update on Marijuana and Cocaine," *The American Journal of Psychiatry* 144 (May 1987), 698.
3. T. N. Robinson, J. D. Killen, C. B. Taylor, "Perspectives on Adolescent Substance Abuse," *Journal of the American Medical Association,* vol. 258, no. 15, 16 Oct. 1987.
4. Dr. Ronald Siegel, interview with author, 28 July 1987.

Further Reading

Books

Brecher, Edward M., and the editors of *Consumers Reports* magazine. *Licit and Illicit Drugs.* Boston: Little, Brown, 1972.

Bressler, Rubin, Morton D. Bogdonoff, and Genell J. Subak-Sharpe, eds. *The Physicians Drugs Manual: Prescription and Nonprescription Drugs.* Garden City, N.Y.: Doubleday, 1981.

Clouet, Doris H., ed. *Phencyclidine: An Update. NIDA Research Monograph 64.* Rockville, Md.: National Institute on Drug Abuse, 1986.

Donlan, John. *I Never Saw the Sunrise.* Minneapolis, Minn.: CompCare Publications, 1977.

Kirsch, M. M. *Designer Drugs.* Minneapolis, Minn.: CompCare, 1986.

Lukas, Scott. *Amphetamines: Danger in the Fast Lane.* New York: Chelsea House, 1985.

Marshall, Shelly. *Young, Sober and Free.* Center City, Minn.: Hazelden, 1978.

Nelson, Jack E., Helen Wallenstein Pearson, Mollie Sayers, and Thomas J. Glynn, eds. *Guide to Drug Abuse Research Terminology.* Vol. 26, *Research Issues.* Rockville, Md.: National Institute on Drug Abuse, 1982.

O'Brien, Robert, and Sidney Cohen. *The Encyclopedia of Drug Abuse.* New York: Facts on File, 1984.

Articles

Adler, Jerry. "Getting High on 'Ecstasy.' " *Newsweek,* 15 Apr. 1985, 96.

Allen, Robert E., Orm Aniline, Ferris N. Pitts, Andrew F. Pitts, and Lane S. Yago. "The Urban Epidemic of Phencyclidine." *Biological Psychiatry* 15, no. 5 (Nov. 1981): 813–17.

American Psychiatric Association. "Position Statement on Psychoactive Substance Use and Dependence: Update on Marijuana and Cocaine." *The American Journal of Psychiatry* 144, no. 5 (May 1987): 698–702.

Ayres, William A., Mary Jo Starsiak, and Phil Sokolay. "The Bogus Drugs: Three Methyl & Alpha Methyl Fentanyl Sold as 'China White.' " *Journal of Psychoactive Drugs* 13, no. 1 (Jan.–Mar. 1981), 91–93.

Baum, Rudy M. "Designer Drugs." *Chemical and Engineering News,* 9 Sept. 1985, 7–16.

Buderi, Robert. "Dr. Detective: How a Trail of Dead Drug Addicts Led to a New Understanding of Parkinson's Disease." *California Magazine* (Feb. 1984), 129.

Chaze, William L. "The Deadly Path of Today's PCP Epidemic." *U.S. News & World Report,* 19 Nov. 1984, 65–67.

Clark, Matt, and Nancy Stadtman. "A Bad Drug's Benefit." *Newsweek,* 9 Dec. 1985.

"Designer Drugs—Murder by Molecule." *U.S. News & World Report,* 5 Aug. 1985, 14.

Dowling, G. P., E. T. McDonough, and R. O. Bost. "Eve and Ecstasy: Report of Five Deaths." *Journal of the American Medical Association* 257, no. 12, 27 Mar. 1987, 1615–17.

Fischman, Joshua. "The Angel Dust Connection." *Psychology Today* (July 1986): 68–69.

Foster, H. M., and N. Narasimhachari. "Phencyclidine in CSF and Serum: A Case of Attempted Filicide By a Mother." *Journal of Clinical Psychiatry* 47, no. 8 (Aug. 1986), 428–29.

Gallagher, Winifred. "The Looming Menace of Designer Drugs." *Discover* (Aug. 1986), 24–34.

Gertz, Kathryn. " 'Hug Drug' Alert: The Agony of Ecstasy." *Harper's Bazaar* (Nov. 1985), 210.

Grinspoon, L. and J. B. Bakalar. "Can Drugs Be Used to Enhance the Psychotherapeutic Process?" *American Journal of Psychotherapy* 40, no. 3. (July 1986), 393–404.

Hymes, Donna. "Coming to Your Senses About Drugs." *Current Health* (Oct. 1986), 19–22.

Isaacs, S. O., P. Martin, and J. A. Washington, Jr. "PCP Abuse: A Close-Up Look at a Growing Problem." *Oral Surgery, Oral Medicine, Oral Pathology* 61, no. 2. (Feb. 1986), 126–29.

Klein, Joe. "The New Drug They Call 'Ecstasy.' " *New York*, 20 May 1985, 38.

Landry, Mim, and David E. Smith. "Crack: Anatomy of an Addiction." *California Nursing Review* 9, no. 2. (March/April 1987), 8.

Lang, John S. "America on Drugs." *U.S. News & World Report*, 28 July 1986, 48–49.

Langston, J. William. "Parkinson's Disease: Current View." *American Family Physician* 35, no. 3 (March 1987), 201–6.

Largent, Dan. "Clandestine Laboratories—The Real Source." Unpublished article by the Clandestine Lab Coordinator, Bureau of Narcotic Enforcement, Department of Justice, California, 1987.

Leikin, J. B., M. Zell, and D. O. Hryhorczuk. "PCP or Cocaine Intoxication?" (letter). *Annals of Emergency Medicine* 16, no. 2 (February 1987), 235–36.

Morgan, John P., Donald R. Wesson, Karoline S. Puder, and David E. Smith. "Duplicitous Drugs: The History and Recent Status of Look-alike Drugs." *Journal of Psychoactive Drugs* 19, no. 1 (Jan.–Mar. 1987), 21–31.

Morse, G. "Angel Dust Clobbers Immune Cells." *Science News,* 7 July 1984, 6.

"PCP: No Angel." *Current Health* (Feb. 1985), 20–22.

Ricaurte, G., G. Bryan, L. Strauss, L. Seiden, and C. Schuster. "Hallu-cinogenic Amphetamine Selectively Destroys Brain Serotonin Nerve Terminals." *Science* 229, no. 4717, 6 Sept. 1985, 986–88.

Roberton, Robert J. "Designer Drugs: The Analog Game." *Narcotics Control Digest,* 3 Apr. 1985, 15.

Roberts, Marjory. "MDMA: Madness Not Ecstasy." *Psychology Today* (June 1986), 14–15.

Schwartz, R. H., and A. Einhorn. "PCP Intoxication in Seven Young Children." *Pediatric Emergency Care* 2, no. 4 (Dec. 1986), 238–41.

Shafer, Jack. "Designer Drugs; By Slightly Altering Molecular Struc-tures, Underground Chemists Are Cooking Up Substitutes for Heroin and Other Drugs." *Science '85* (March 1985), 60–67.

———. "Designer Drugs: America's Deadly New High-Tech Highs." *Designer Drugs* (April 1984), 1–3.

———. "MDMA: Psychedelic Drug Faces Regulation." *Psychology Today* (May 1985), 68–69.

Shulgin, Alexander T. "Profiles of Psychedelic Drugs." *Journal of Psyche-delic Drugs* 8, no. 4 (Oct.–Dec, 1976): 331.

Siegel, R. K. "Chemical Ecstasies." *Omni* (Aug. 1985), 29.

———. "New Trends in Drug Use Among Youth in California." *Bulle-tin of Narcotics* (Apr.–Sept. 1985), 29.

———. "MDMA: Nonmedical Use and Intoxication." *Journal of Psycho-active Drugs* 18, no. 4 (Oct.–Dec. 1986), 349–54.

Smart, R. G., and E. M. Adlaf. "Drug Abuse Patterns of Adolescents: The Past Decade." *Social Science Medicine* 23, no. 7 (1986), 717–19.

Smith, David E., and Richard Seymour. "Clarification of 'Designer Drugs.'" *U.S. Journal* (Nov. 1985), 9.

Strauss, Hal. "From Crack to Ecstasy." *American Health* (June 1987), 50–54.

"The Sweet Stuff: An Update on Artificial Sweeteners." *Current Health* (Jan. 1985), 16–19.

Taylor, Ronald A. "Uncovering New Truths About the Country's No. 1 Menace." *U.S. News & World Report,* 28 July 1986, 50.

Wallis, Claudia. "Surprising Clue to Parkinson's; A California Street Drug Is Linked to the Disease." *Time,* 8 Apr. 1985, 61–62.

Wright, J. M., R. A. Wall, T. L. Perry, and D. W. Paty. "Chronic Parkinsonism Secondary to Intranasal Administration of a Product of Meperidine Analog Synthesis." *New England Journal of Medicine* 310, no. 5, 2 Feb. 1984, 325.

Zerkin, Leif E., and Jeffrey H. Novey, eds. "MDMA: Proceedings of the Conference." *Journal of Psychoactive Drugs* 18, no. 4 (Oct.–Dec. 1986).

Ziporyn, T. "A Growing Industry and Menace: Makeshift Laboratory's Designer Drugs." *Journal of the American Medical Association,* 256, no. 22, 12 Dec. 1986, 3061–63.

Reports

California Legislature, Senate Select Committee on Drug and Alcohol Abuse. *Interim Hearings on Clandestine Laboratories/Designer Drugs.* 5 Nov. 1985. Sacramento, Calif.: State of California, 1985.

Drug Enforcement Administration. *Drugs of Abuse.* Washington: U.S. Department of Justice, 1985.

Johnston, Lloyd D., Patrick M. O'Malley, and Jerald G. Bachman. The University of Michigan Institute for Social Research. *Highlights from Drugs and American High School Students, 1975–1983.* Rockville, Md.: National Institute on Drug Abuse, 1984.

National Institute on Drug Abuse. *Drug Abuse Trends and Research Issues: Community Epidemiology Work Group Proceedings, December 1986.* Rockville, Md.: National Institute on Drug Abuse, 1987.

————. *Highlights: 1985 National Household Survey on Drug Abuse.* Rockville, Md.: National Institute on Drug Abuse, 1986.

————. *Population Projections Based on the National Survey on Drug Abuse, 1982.* Rockville, Md.: National Institute on Drug Abuse, 1983.

————. *Statistical Series, Annual Data 1985.* Rockville, Md.: National Institute on Drug Abuse, 1986.

National Narcotics Intelligence Consumers Committee. *The Supply of Illicit Drugs to the United States from Foreign and Domestic Sources in 1985 and 1986.* Washington: U.S. Department of Justice, 1987.

U.S. House of Representatives, Congressional Hearing Before the Subcommittee on Crime of the Committee on the Judiciary. *Designer Drugs.* 1 May 1986. Washington: U.S. Government Printing Office, 1986.

U.S. Senate, Congressional Hearing Before the Subcommittee on Children, Family, Drugs and Alcoholism of the Committee on Labor and Human Resources. *Designer Drugs.* 25 July 1985. Washington: U.S. Government Printing Office, 1985.

Western States Information Network. *The 1983 California Clandestine Laboratory Situation.* Sacramento, Calif.: Western States Information Network, 1984.

Television

"Designer Drugs." *Phil Donahue Show* transcript no. 09116, Sept. 1986.

"The Frozen Addict." *Nova.* Originally aired on Feb. 18, 1986, this program is aired on PBS at various times.

Index

Tweak bugs, 40, 44

About the Author

Michele McCormick is a California-based freelance writer who has written for magazines and newspapers in this country and overseas. In addition to her articles covering a broad range of current issues, Ms. McCormick has written extensively about subjects of interest to the military. A book compilation of her military-oriented essays, titled *Polishing Up the Brass,* was published in 1988.

Ms. McCormick currently lives near Sacramento with her Army officer husband, Don McCormick.